KT-484-219

Coping with a Mid-life Crisis
Derek Milne

Coping with Polycystic Ovary Syndrome
Christine Craggs-Hinton

Coping with Postnatal Depression
Sandra L. Wheatley

Coping with SAD
Fiona Marshall and Peter Cheevers

Coping with Snoring and Sleep Apnoea
Jill Eckersley

Coping with Strokes
Dr Tom Smith

Coping with Suicide
Maggie Helen

Coping with Teenagers
Sarah Lawson

Coping with Thyroid Problems
Dr Joan Gomez

Coping with Thrush
Caroline Clayton

Curing Arthritis – The Drug-Free Way
Margaret Hills

Curing Arthritis – More Ways to a Drug-Free Life
Margaret Hills

Curing Arthritis Diet Book
Margaret Hills

Curing Arthritis Exercise Book
Margaret Hills and Janet Horwood

Depression at Work
Vicky Maud

Depressive Illness
Dr Tim Cantopher

Eating for a Healthy Heart
Robert Povey, Jacqui Morrell and Rachel Povey

Effortless Exercise
Dr Caroline Shreeve

Fertility
Julie Reid

The Fibromyalgia Healing Diet
Christine Craggs-Hinton

Free Your Life from Fear
Jenny Hare

Getting a Good Night's Sleep
Fiona Johnston

Heal the Hurt: How to Forgive and Move On
Dr Ann Macaskill

Heart Attacks – Prevent and Survive
Dr Tom Smith

Help Your Child Get Fit Not Fat
Jan Hurst and Sue Hubberstey

Helping Children Cope with Attention Deficit Disorder
Dr Patricia Gilbert

Helping Children Cope with Change and Loss
Rosemary Wells

Helping Children Cope with Grief
Rosemary Wells

Helping Children Get the Most from School
Sarah Lawson

How to Accept Yourself
Dr Windy Dryden

How to Be Your Own Best Friend
Dr Paul Hauck

How to Cope with Bulimia
Dr Joan Gomez

How to Cope with Difficult People
Alan Houel and Christian Godefroy

How to Improve Your Confidence
Dr Kenneth Hambly

How to Keep Your Cholesterol in Check
Dr Robert Povey

How to Make Yourself Miserable
Dr Windy Dryden

How to Stand up for Yourself
Dr Paul Hauck

How to Stick to a Diet
Deborah Steinberg and Dr Windy Dryden

How to Stop Worrying
Dr Frank Tallis

How to Untangle Your Emotional Knots
Dr Windy Dryden and Jack Gordon

Hysterectomy
Suzie Hayman

The Irritable Bowel Diet Book
Rosemary Nicol

Is HRT Right for You?
Dr Anne MacGregor

Letting Go of Anxiety and Depression
Dr Windy Dryden

Lifting Depression the Balanced Way
Dr Lindsay Corrie

Overcoming Common Problems Series

Living with Alzheimer's
Tom Smith

Living with Asperger Syndrome
Joan Gomez

Living with Asthma
Dr Robert Youngson

Living with Autism
Fiona Marshall

Living with Crohn's Disease
Dr Joan Gomez

Living with Diabetes
Dr Joan Gomez

Living with Fibromyalgia
Christine Craggs-Hinton

Living with Food Intolerance
Alex Gazzola

Living with Grief
Dr Tony Lake

Living with Heart Disease
Victor Marks, Dr Monica Lewis and
Dr Gerald Lewis

Living with High Blood Pressure
Dr Tom Smith

Living with Hughes Syndrome
Triona Holden

Living with Nut Allergies
Karen Evennett

Living with Osteoarthritis
Dr Patricia Gilbert

Living with Osteoporosis
Dr Joan Gomez

Living with Rheumatoid Arthritis
Philippa Pigache

Living with Sjögren's Syndrome
Sue Dyson

Losing a Baby
Sarah Ewing

Losing a Child
Linda Hurcombe

Make Up or Break Up: Making the Most of Your Marriage
Mary Williams

Making Friends with Your Stepchildren
Rosemary Wells

Overcoming Anger
Dr Windy Dryden

Overcoming Anxiety
Dr Windy Dryden

Overcoming Back Pain
Dr Tom Smith

Overcoming Depression
Dr Windy Dryden and Sarah Opie

Overcoming Guilt
Dr Windy Dryden

Overcoming Impotence
Mary Williams

Overcoming Jealousy
Dr Windy Dryden

Overcoming Procrastination
Dr Windy Dryden

Overcoming Shame
Dr Windy Dryden

Overcoming Your Addictions
Dr Windy Dryden and
Dr Walter Matweychuk

The PMS Diet Book
Karen Evennett

Rheumatoid Arthritis
Mary-Claire Mason and Dr Elaine Smith

The Self-Esteem Journal
Alison Waines

Shift Your Thinking, Change Your Life
Mo Shapiro

Stress and Depression in Children and Teenagers
Vicky Maud

Stress at Work
Mary Hartley

Ten Steps to Positive Living
Dr Windy Dryden

Think Your Way to Happiness
Dr Windy Dryden and Jack Gordon

The Traveller's Good Health Guide
Ted Lankester

Understanding Obsessions and Compulsions
Dr Frank Tallis

When Someone You Love Has Depression
Barbara Baker

Work–Life Balance
Gordon and Ronni Lamont

Your Man's Health
Fiona Marshall

Overcoming Common Problems

Help Your Child Get Fit Not Fat

Jan Hurst and Sue Hubberstey

sheldon PRESS

First published in Great Britain in 2005
Sheldon Press
36 Causton Street
London SW1P 4ST

British Library Cataloguing-in-Publication Data

A catalogue record for this book is available from the British Library

ISBN 0–85969–934–X

1 3 5 7 9 10 8 6 4 2

Typeset by Deltatype Limited, Birkenhead, Merseyside
Printed in Great Britain by
Ashford Colour Press

Contents

Introduction   xi

1 The facts, the problems, the influences   1
2 Peer pressure, school lunches, vegetarianism,
   faddy eaters   9
3 Family meals, the pressure to be thin, bullying   19
4 Creating an invisible fitness programme   29
5 Avoiding pushy parent syndrome, introducing
   non-competitive activities, puppy fat, 'fat camps'   39
6 The onset of puberty, eating disorders   49
7 Alienation, smoking, drinking, illegal drug-taking   59
8 The couch potato, loss of interest in sport,
   activities to do together   69
9 Lethargy, depression   79
10 The future, eating together, refusing to be
   influenced by the media, taking a moral stand   89

Conclusion   97

*For our mothers – Gladys Parrock and
Doris White – who fed us well*

Introduction

'The fastest growing form of malnutrition' is how obesity has been described by the World Health Organization and it seems that no culture in the world is immune. More people are now suffering from the effects of overeating than from hunger, and obesity has become a real threat to future generations.

The facts paint an alarming picture. In the USA 33 per cent of its adult population is obese but European countries are fast catching up and in the UK the percentage of people who are overweight or obese has more than doubled over the past 30 years. If we allow these trends to continue it is estimated that at least one third of adults will be obese by 2020.

Life expectancy has been steadily increasing, as we have found cures and treatments for diseases such as tuberculosis and pneumonia from which the young as well as the old commonly died. Now it seems that this trend is in serious danger of being reversed. It is predicted that thousands of people will suffer and die prematurely from the diseases associated with obesity. Overweight has been linked to heart disease, several different types of cancer, diabetes and asthma. Furthermore, it seems that people are beginning to exhibit the problems associated with being overweight at a much earlier age. Heart problems have been identified in children as young as six years old and doctors have begun to express alarm at seeing in children for the first time Type 2 diabetes, the form of diabetes which has in the past only been associated with overweight in mature adults.

There is also a serious risk factor for expectant mothers. A review of maternal health showed that a third of women who die as the result of complications in pregnancy or childbirth are obese.

Obesity has negative psychological effects, too, and can result in low self-esteem, social stigma and a generally poorer quality of life. Overweight children are frequently bullied and teased at school. Our society has also developed an obsession with body image which leads many young people, especially teenage girls, into eating disorders. This affects the adolescent's social behaviour, school performance and emotional health and it should be of concern to everyone that in the UK a record number of children are now being prescribed antidepressants. This could have serious repercussions for society at large. Unhappy people are much more likely to drink heavily or take drugs.

The social implications of having a young population with all sorts of health problems are obvious. It is clearly important that young people are nurtured carefully so that they may become healthy adults and contributors to the common good. After all, our society runs on the belief that there is a fit working population available to support the rapidly growing number of older people who are no longer working. If action isn't taken now the results could be catastrophic for all of us.

1

The facts, the problems, the influences

How much is our lifestyle to blame for the growing rise in obesity? None of us can afford to ignore the fact that we are faced with a worldwide crisis in chronic diseases linked to poor eating habits and lack of exercise, albeit one which in general terms has been self-inflicted. So much in the lifestyle we choose to have today seems to conspire to prevent children from developing good eating habits. It has been estimated that children and young people (those aged four to 18) in England are eating more than twice the amount of fat they need, more than twice the salt needed and only a quarter of the fruit and vegetables required for good health. Eating food overloaded with sugar and fats while taking little or no exercise results, inevitably, in more and more of our young people becoming overweight, or obese.

Eating habits and exercise

Eating habits have changed drastically in many families over the past few decades. We all eat far more processed and prepared meals and order takeaways on a regular basis. Some of us no longer have the patience or the time to cook, shop or even eat leisurely. In the 1960s it took about two and a half hours to prepare a meal; now it's more likely to be about 15 minutes. We are bombarded with advertisements for family meals which can be prepared in a matter of minutes, often simply being reheated in a microwave oven.

We also tend to eat out quite frequently and restaurant food tends to have more calories than home-cooked meals. Food consumption has become a major preoccupation and far from overindulgence being a source of shame it is actively encouraged in fast-food outlets, where there is much emphasis on 'eating as much as you can' for a set price.

1

Portions of food have grown much larger and coffee, tea and fizzy drinks come in large as well as regular sizes, but these are intended to be consumed as quickly as possible.

We also snack in a way unthought of in past generations. It is possible to be constantly grazing throughout the day on things such as crisps and chocolate bars. Often children get conflicting messages when these products are promoted by a favourite sports star or entertainer.

If you recognize some of these behaviour patterns in your own family or suspect that your child is carrying more weight than he should, it's time for some radical changes.

Parental denial can be an issue, especially if the parents themselves are overweight and unfit. Don't kid yourself that your child doesn't look fat. You may believe that he is simply going through a stage and suffering 'puppy fat'. Or you perhaps believe you have an active child, particularly if you are not very active yourself. But you have to ask yourself what that means.

Make a list of the physical activities your child is involved in each day. Does he just ride his bike to his friend down the road and spend the rest of the time with him in front of the PlayStation? All children and adults should be having a period of moderately intense physical activity every day of the week. At least 30 minutes is recommended for adults and one hour for children. This does not mean you have to spend part of every day at the gym: a brisk walk will suffice. It seems an undemanding target, and yet many people find even this impossible in their busy schedule.

Children need to understand the links between a healthy diet, regular exercise and their physical and emotional health. It may be a cliché to say 'we are what we eat' but good food does help us feel good about ourselves. Poor quality food may, initially, seem very tasty but, in fact, too much of it can leave you feeling lethargic and depressed.

Your child's early experience of food will help shape his eating habits in early life, but we have changed how we eat as much as what we eat and have drifted a long way from the three regular meals a day – breakfast, lunch and dinner – shared by the whole family around the dinner table. Often members eat different meals and separately, in their bedrooms or in front of the television. Some families have even dispensed with a dining table or have turned the dining room into a study or hobby room and, although many of us spend vast amounts of money installing beautiful fitted kitchens, this does not necessarily mean they are places where we spend much time preparing wholesome meals these days.

One country where obesity is not yet a national problem is France. The French have a diet high in cream, butter, cheese and meat but only 10 per cent of the adult population is obese, a comparatively small figure compared with the USA, the home of fast food. The French live longer and have lower death rates from coronary heart disease. They enjoy their food; in fact they are passionate about it and see cooking as a pleasure rather than a chore. In France, 76 per cent of the meals eaten have been prepared at home, the favourite place to have both lunch and dinner is at home and the great majority eat together at the family table, rather than standing up, or in the workplace, or in front of the television. They regularly eat three meals a day, allowing around two hours for lunch, and tend to buy food on a daily basis rather than filling a huge chest freezer with ready-prepared meals for a month. They shop at local markets for bread, meat, fish and vegetables. The family meal is an event, which is taken at a slow, leisurely pace. While we are not suggesting that we should emulate a different culture (which is itself beginning to change, anyway), and start insisting on two hours for lunch and campaigning for a baker, fishmonger and butcher on every street corner, we can train ourselves to think differently about the way in which our families eat and live together.

Try a little experiment next time you return from the supermarket trip. Sit down with the till receipt and add up everything you bought that is a snack, sweet, fizzy drink or convenience food. You are likely to be amazed at just how much money goes on the things that supermarkets would have us believe are cheap and are often offered as part of bargain, two-for-one deals. When you've recovered from this shock, take a look at your petrol bills for one month and work out how much of that was spent on ferrying the children from one friend's house to another and from making trips which you know in your heart of hearts you could have easily walked. Now, consider extending your experiment to not buying any of those snacks for a month and not making those little car journeys. The money you save could be spent on a trip with the children to your nearest bowling alley or in trying a restaurant you might not have considered before. A healthy, fit life for the family does not mean a boring, mundane life; exactly the opposite, in fact, and your month's experiment could prove to be life-changing for all the family.

The need for exercise

It is easy to see why a combination of well-balanced, nutritious meals and the chance to participate in some regular and enjoyable physical exercise is essential if our children are to grow into healthy, robust individuals. But, increasingly, we have been limiting our children's access to physical exercise as well as to healthy food. The pattern of children's play has changed dramatically in the past few decades. Once upon a time the streets were full of children who, when they were not at school, were skipping, playing hopscotch, riding their bikes or roller skating, but these are now increasingly rare sights. The majority of children and teenagers spend their leisure time indoors, watching television, playing computer games and chatting or texting on their mobile phones. Technology now dominates the life of the average teenager.

A former director of the Children's Play Council has spoken of the 'outdoor' child being at risk of extinction. He claimed that in a single generation the 'home habitat' of a typical eight-year-old – the area in which children are able to travel on their own – has shrunk to one-ninth of its former size. It has been estimated that more and more children are failing to have the hour of physical exercise a day recommended by the World Health Organization. We have also reduced public play space, which is now at a premium. School playing fields have been sold off with thoughtless abandon and for every acre of land in England used for playgrounds over 80 acres are now given over to golf courses! Children have fewer and fewer opportunities to take a brisk walk or a cycle ride to school; instead they are ferried everywhere by car and consequently these so-called 'battery reared' children lack the confidence to go out alone.

Parents drive their children everywhere with the best of intentions. They feel the streets are unsafe for their children to go out alone and believe they are putting them at risk of abduction. This belief is more perception than reality. In fact there is no greater risk of a child being abducted and killed than there was a generation ago. It's also a fact – perhaps unpalatable to some parents – that children need to learn how to negotiate the traffic on the streets rather than simply viewing it through a car window. It is significant that the highest rate of child accidents occurs in children over 11, the age at which they are most likely to begin travelling unescorted to school for the first time in their lives. Lack of practice at being a pedestrian makes them feel insecure and, therefore, makes them vulnerable.

Unfortunately, many schools have also limited the opportunities for children to participate in healthy exercise as there has been a reduction in the amount of physical education and sport on offer. Only two hours of organized physical activity a week is planned into the busy National Curriculum in the UK and, given the demands of so many other subjects, teachers often find it difficult even to deliver this. Half of primary schools in England have cut PE lessons by 30 minutes per week and some schools are reported to have only 12 hours of PE a year!

None of us can afford to be complacent. Most of us are

capable of overeating and of becoming overweight. There has to be a concerted effort by parents, schools, health professionals and the government to take action to reverse the trend. We can't pretend that it is going to be easy. The habits of irregular eating, processed food and taking the car rather than walking or cycling are so entrenched in our lives that it will take much hard work to make changes.

If a child is to lose weight it must be a family affair, not just the child who eats more healthily and takes more exercise. It is vital that parents present themselves as healthy role models and adopt a whole family approach to taking control and changing lifestyle and eating habits. If you and most of the other members of your family are significantly overweight you are less likely to notice that your child has a problem, but wanting the best for your child includes giving him the opportunity to live a healthy lifestyle.

Some people believe that the food industry should be more strictly regulated and the government has begun to tackle the problem of direct advertising to children and taken steps to enforce companies to make labelling clearer on tinned and pre-packaged food so that we really are aware of what we are buying.

School meals

The government also has a role to play in ensuring that a healthy environment is provided in schools and that nutritious lunches are offered rather than an excess of food with a high fat, salt or sugar content. In many local education authorities school cooks have become redundant. Meals have ceased to be cooked in the school kitchen but are instead delivered as prepared packs which simply have to be heated up. Even the vegetables come ready chopped.

Good practice is evident in some schools where there has been a move back to freshly cooked meals and where staff are doing their best to devise menus which will tempt the children to eat a healthier and more varied diet. But the impression given is that in most schools enormous amounts of burgers, sausages and chips are being dished up at lunchtime and washed down with fizzy drinks from the school vending machine. Even if salad and fresh vegetables are on offer they are usually presented in an unimaginative way which has no appeal for children.

There is some evidence that the growth in school breakfast clubs is having beneficial effects and helping children to make a good start to the day. These were initially intended to ensure that children from poorer families had a nourishing breakfast but they are now more usually open to all pupils in the school. Breakfast is acknowledged as the most important meal of the day yet we know that many children have nothing at all to eat first thing in the morning, a habit that is continued in the teenage years, especially among girls. Anything that encourages our children to have a proper breakfast must be welcomed, especially as it has been shown to significantly improve concentration and academic performance.

Breakfast clubs can be a real boon to working parents who don't have time in the morning for arguments about breakfast at home. They can also help to improve school attendance and punctuality. The word 'club' emphasizes the social aspects and because many children will enjoy meeting their friends there and enjoying a meal together, they are encouraged to get out of bed earlier and off to school. Sharing breakfast with each other and possibly with members of staff can be a pleasant experience and a good start to the day.

Other initiatives in schools have also shown positive results. Initial research on the effects of the free fruit scheme in nurseries and primary schools, whereby every child under the age of seven is given at least one piece of fruit per day, shows that this has encouraged children to eat more fruit in and out of school hours. The challenge will be for parents to sustain that habit if or when the initiative comes to an end.

There are enlightened schools which are now ensuring that

the children have five minutes of exercise before classes; others are providing the children with bottled water throughout the day. Children are much more likely to drink bottled water than use the old-fashioned water fountains, which are often situated in the lavatories! In some primary school playgrounds you will find supervisors teaching children to play the type of ball games and skipping games which previous generations knew almost instinctively and time and money is being spent on making playground equipment more interesting and challenging. Other schools are trying to offer children a wider selection of sports in order to make physical activities more attractive to those who don't enjoy the traditional games. While football is still a favourite sport for boys, many teenage girls are reluctant to sweat it out on the netball or hockey pitch but may be encouraged to take part in aerobic exercise or some form of dancing.

Changes have to be made to ensure that this generation of children grow up into healthy, well-balanced adults. As we have discussed, all elements of society carry some responsibility for making the necessary improvements but it is your role as parent which is pivotal. It is only with your assistance and by your example that the tide can turn. The revolution starts here.

2
Peer pressure, school lunches, vegetarianism, faddy eaters

Outside influences on your child's diet

As soon as your child starts school she will be subjected to outside influences with regard to what she eats. There will be discussion among school friends on favourite foods and dislikes and when your child is invited to her friends' homes she will also sample snacks and drinks that may not meet with your approval. It is important to keep a sense of balance with regard to what your child eats when she is not with you: if you know that one particular friend has unrestricted access to junk food and fizzy drinks and that your child shares in this when she visits, it would be a good idea to pay extra attention to providing a nutritious meal when she returns home and to supervising tooth brushing that night. It is not helpful, however, to openly criticize the food and drink that is on offer when your child visits her friend, as this undermines the home and family life of the other child and places your child in the difficult position of suffering split loyalties between enjoying the company of her friend and eating and drinking as you would wish. The importance and value of your child learning to socialize and bond with other children should take precedence over any occasional lapses in good eating habits.

One way of minimizing this problem is to ensure that your child's friends pay plenty of visits to your home so that you are in control of the eating and drinking. If you are at home yourself then this could entail a baking session that you, your child and her friend enjoy together, or you could simply have a selection of fruit, dips, oatcakes and other healthy and satisfying snacks ready for when the children arrive home from school.

If you are working and your child and her friend are looked after by a childminder or nanny when they finish school you could prepare the snacks in advance and point them out to the adult in charge if they are coming to your home. However, if the childminder takes your child to her house after school, you will need to remain tactful at all times and, providing her choice of snacks is not too extreme, you will simply have to balance your child's intake when you are in charge.

It can be even more frustrating and difficult when your child is routinely given what you consider to be unhealthy food by other members of your family – her grandparents, your former partner, a step-parent or other well-meaning relations. When this happens you need to remind yourself that food should never become a battleground, in any shape or form, because your child will inevitably pick up on the problem, however diplomatic you feel you are being in her presence. You may believe that other adults are trying to win your child's affection by plying her with sweets and chips, and that this forces you into the mould of 'boring parent', worrying about your child's long-term well-being. But by trying to restrict her intake of fat and sugar, you know that you are acting in the best interests of your child and the most enjoyable treat you can provide for her comes in the form of your time and affection – these things far outweigh the momentary gratification provided by a chocolate bar.

Advertising

In addition to the influence of peers and other family members your child will increasingly be targeted by the media once she has reached the age where she can voice an opinion on what she would like to watch on television. The advertising that is placed before, after and in between the programmes your child is likely to enjoy includes material designed to promote foods that appeal to children and are high in fat and sugar. The debate between the medical establishment and the advertising industry on the influence such advertising might have over our children's future health prospects is ongoing. Any attempt to prevent your child from being exposed to this kind of advertising is likely to become very stressful for both of you and is unlikely to work. However, you can sit down with your child and casually enlighten her as to what such advertising is all about. You do not need to lecture but merely to point out in simple terms that the advertising is paid for by large companies who are interested in making lots of money. The more they can persuade people to eat their products, the more money they make and the more they can advertise. It is surprising how quickly young children can become aware of how this type of product promotion works and once they are aware of it they are likely to realize when they are being 'sold' to.

In recent years snack food manufacturers have hit upon the idea of selling to both children and parents through the concept of buying the product and saving tokens for school equipment. The notion of buying the snack to achieve something worthwhile is a tempting one but not if it means we all end up eating more junk food than ever. This is a particularly cynical ploy and one worth objecting to. If your child's school has a collection bin for product tokens or has sent home a letter asking you to save crisp packets towards school equipment then you might consider getting in touch with like-minded parents to challenge this at your next PTA or governors' meeting. A new computer for the school should not come at the cost of the children's health and well-being.

A less sophisticated, but none the less effective, tug on our children's indirect buying power comes in the form of free gifts attached to packs of cereal or the promise of a free gift if pack tokens are collected. Annoyingly, it is usually the chocolate-coated, sugar-loaded cereal that contains the free gift, never the bag of porridge oats. One way around this obstacle is to avoid the supermarket aisle that contains these temptations, if you are shopping with your child or, if you

11

can, shop alone. There is one exception to avoiding products with 'an ulterior motive' such as getting a free gift, and that is Fair Trade products. If your child knows that one day each week, to be chosen by her, is 'sweetie day', she is less likely to demand sweets on other days, and if you buy a Fair Trade chocolate bar and tell her why you are choosing this particular product, then you will be on the road to encouraging an 'ethical' attitude towards food.

The lunch box versus the school meal

In the light of widespread concern over children's long-term health prospects, many schools are reintroducing a healthier lunch menu. However, salads, vegetables and fruit are frequently offered alongside chips and burgers and your child will be making her choice among friends who may be tempted by the less healthy options. If your child prefers to have a school meal and the menu is less than satisfactory, it is worth pursuing the route of the PTA and governors to campaign for an improvement. Most schools e-mail parents or post each week's menu on the school noticeboard in advance.

If your child chooses to take a packed lunch there is a lot you can do to ensure that she enjoys a healthy midday meal.

The trimmings

It may sound odd to pay attention to the box itself, before discussing what goes in it, but appearances are more important to children than most adults care to acknowledge. You are more likely to receive a favourable uptake on your packed lunch if you provide an attractive container and appropriate cutlery and napkin (or wet wipe), where necessary. Choose a rigid lunch box to protect the contents and only buy a box with a decorative theme if it is age appropriate and your child approves. Some boxes contain freezer pads to help keep food cool but these usually take up a lot of room in the box and you can keep food cool in other ways (more on this later). Boxes also come divided into compartments, which seems a useful idea until you try to force food into each slot. Stick with a basic design which is easy to clean and label the box with a food marker pen inside and out. Buying a good supply of plain paper napkins, small plastic spoons and transparent freezer food bags at the start of each term will help keep you organized.

Lunch box tips

- Choosing a wholemeal roll provides extra roughage and is more filling than white. Your child may dislike grain and nuts, 'because of the bits', so start with plain, soft rolls and gradually introduce variations.
- Butter/margarine can become 'sweaty' so don't automatically spread it unless your child loves it. Try a thin slick of mayonnaise to provide a creamy taste or add extra lettuce to prevent filling tasting dry. Thinly sliced cheese is a good choice of filling, as is tuna mixed with a tablespoon of mayonnaise. Do not overload the filling as it will create a mess and children are easily put off from eating what appears to them to be a huge portion.
- Spears of celery/carrot stay crunchy if washed and packed in clingfilm. Cut into easily manageable sticks.
- Yogurt/fromage frais in tubes does away with 'messy tub syndrome' and acts as cooler sticks if pre-frozen.
- A transparent beaker of diluted juice is preferable to concentrates or carbonated drinks in terms of tooth decay. Calories/energy should always be provided by slow-release foods rather than liquids. The beaker can be frozen overnight to keep the lunch box cool.
- A ready-peeled satsuma is less likely to be overlooked and it will stay juicy if packed in plastic.
- Try making homemade cereal bars – it's not that time-consuming and your child can help you make them! She is more likely to eat what she has prepared, and you can control the ingredients and save money.

13

Things to avoid

- White bread – this has had the fibre removed to make it more palatable – why bother?
- Sandwich fillings/paste – heavy on additives to provide flavour and contain the cheapest bits of meat or fish.
- Crisps and other food labelled 'low fat' – fat is usually replaced by sugar or chemical binding agents to hold ingredients together. Constantly eating 'low fat' products will not educate taste buds to enjoy 'real' food. Give good-quality crisps once or twice a week.
- Concentrated juice – corrodes tooth enamel and does not provide enough water.
- Cartons of fruit dessert – contain little fruit, lots of refined sugar and are not filling.
- Manufactured cereal bars – these contain little 'slow release' energy and lots of sugar. They are often higher in calories than chocolate bars and are always more expensive.
- Bananas are a perfect source of energy but are lunch box nightmares – if they aren't squished they turn black and ooze over other food.

Vegetarianism

If you are a vegetarian it should come easily to you to provide a balanced diet for your child that includes all the protein and iron-rich food that growing children require. There is no reason why a vegetarian family should eat any less healthily than meat-eaters; indeed you are less likely to succumb to the type of convenience foods that are heavily laden with fat, sugar and chemical additives. However, if your child develops a dislike of meat or takes to the idea of becoming vegetarian at an early age, while you and the rest of the family remain meat-eaters, you will need to give extra consideration to the nutritional content of family meals.

It is quite easy to fall into the trap, when you are trying to cater for different likes and dislikes within the family, of bulking up the vegetarian's plate with extra bread, potatoes and pasta to compensate for the missing meat or fish content of the meal. Unbalanced meals that rely heavily on carbohydrates can lead to unwanted weight gain, and a lack of iron (found readily in red meat) can make a child tired and lacking in energy. This, in turn, leads to the child cutting down on physical activity, which, again, precipitates weight gain and loss of both physical fitness and mental alertness. To compensate for the absence of meat you will need to provide iron in the form of pulses and, if your child is not a vegan, egg yolks. Protein can be gained from cheese, milk, nuts, cereal grains, rice, seeds and pulses. It is vitally important not to ridicule your child's choice, even if she has always enjoyed meat in the past and you feel she is being influenced by friends rather than moral issues. Food and mealtimes must remain 'neutral' and a healthy attitude towards eating and enjoying food is paramount.

Faddy eating

Starting school often triggers other changes in attitude regarding food. Going to school heralds feelings of greater independence in children and this is often tested at the meal table. If she has not done so before, your child may now begin refusing certain foods, even those that were favourites a short time ago. Most parents worry when this starts to happen that their child will suffer some kind of nutritional deficiency or remain a fussy, faddy eater for the rest of its life, but this is simply not the case. Refusing foods or only eating a limited amount of certain foods is a sure-fire way of their gaining your attention and ensuring that you care.

It is difficult when this happens not to react with coaxing, bribery, threats or rewards, but taking any or all of these routes is sure to turn mealtimes into a battle of wills and could induce an unhealthy attitude towards food in your child. If your child learns to use food and eating as a power tool it could quite easily become an even bigger problem when she's older. Many overweight adults cite being made to finish meals by their parents when they were little as the reason for their weight problems, as do many anorexics. The whole issue of food refusal and faddiness can be very stressful, so you might try defusing the situation and your feelings by eating a picnic outside when the weather permits, going to a café or restaurant occasionally, and inviting friends and family round to eat en masse. In this way you will be showing your child that food and eating are part of enjoyable social events and relieving yourself of some of the tension involved in this phase.

It is very important, if your child eats earlier than you and other members of the family, to always sit down and accompany his meal, even if you only have a cup of coffee. Your child should not be left alone to eat while you get on with chores, or placed in front of the TV with a plate of food, because then enjoying the food is likely to be secondary to watching TV or to getting back to what he was doing before you called him to eat.

Tips for dealing with fussy eaters and food refusers

- If your child refuses a certain food, clear it away without comment – he is snubbing the food, not you.
- Don't allow your child to fill up with snacks and fizzy drinks between meals.
- While your child is going through this 'stage' keep food preparation and expense to a minimum so that you avoid becoming resentful at the waste of time and money.
- Put less food on your child's plate.
- Set a good example and ask older children to help by not being fussy at the table.
- Invite your child's friends round to eat, particularly if you know they are 'healthy' eaters.
- Never use food as a bribe, reward or punishment and never let your child see you are worried or angry over his eating.

16

A word about allergy

Allergies in childhood have been increasing over the last 20 years and if your child seems consistently to show an adverse reaction to a particular food or foods, it is worth investigating further via your GP or an allergy specialist. Food allergy is a complex area, but the commonest food allergies in children are to cows' milk, eggs, wheat, soya, peanuts, tree nuts, fish and shellfish, and some fruits. Symptoms of food allergy vary greatly from child to child and in the degree of severity. They can include facial swelling and flushing, a blotchy, itchy rash, a feeling that the throat is swelling up, breathing difficulties, wheezing, nausea and vomiting, colic or diarrhoea. Most serious – but luckily rare – is anaphylaxis, a very severe reaction to the offending food substance which if untreated can be life-threatening.

However, there is much that parents can do to minimize the effects of allergy and to make children more comfortable. (See *Coping with Childhood Allergies* by Jill Eckersley, also published by Sheldon Press, which gives information on how to manage childhood allergic conditions.)

Encouraging cooking skills

One proven method of ensuring that your child takes a healthy interest in food and gets to eat a wide variety of healthy produce is to encourage him to cook. Planning a menu together and allowing him to contribute his likes and dislikes is empowering for him and leads, logically, to him eating the result. Before you begin you need to choose a day or days when you are less rushed than usual, perhaps at weekends to start with, so that you do not fall into the trap of 'taking over'. Very young children will enjoy having their own apron and smaller utensils with which to prepare food and, if you manage to keep this routine going, you will find that older children tend to use their time in the kitchen with you as a time to talk over worries and discuss their concerns as you cook.

17

If your child wants to attempt something you consider rather ambitious you will need to modify the recipe without curbing his enthusiasm. And while wielding large kitchen knives might be something to be avoided, you could still let your child cut up herbs with small scissors, grate cheese, mash potatoes and make pastry with his hands. Enjoying the textures, smells and tastes of recipes forms a large part of accepting a wider diet and really enjoying meal times.

Grow your own

If you want your child to develop a real appreciation of vegetables and fruit, of course, the answer lies in growing them yourself. You may feel you don't have time for an allotment or large vegetable garden but 'half-plots' are usually available at council allotment sites and this would provide your child with plenty of opportunity to play in the open air (ideal if you have a very small garden or none at all) and to sample the wonder of growing something from seed from an early age. The exercise involved in digging and planting is also ideal for children who are less than keen on competitive sports and every hour spent at the allotment is one hour less in front of the TV or computer screen. Even if you can't contemplate an allotment you can grow tomatoes, sweetcorn, runner beans and much more besides in a small garden or even on a balcony and it's guaranteed that your child will want to eat what he grows.

3

Family meals, the pressure to be thin, bullying

We have already mentioned how traditional family eating habits have changed and how, in some cases, some children never sit down to eat at the table with their parents.

It's easy to see how the habit of families regularly eating together can be lost. Working parents may arrive home at different times of the day, especially if they work shifts or flexi-time. Many children now have a number of after-school activities and may be dashing out just as Mum and Dad get home. Young children who are at nursery or with a childminder may well have their last meal of the day there, and older children who are at home alone after school will probably raid the fridge for snacks and won't have an appetite for a full family meal later on. Often, members of the family are so busy that they barely have time to speak to each other let alone sit down and eat a leisurely meal.

Instead, eating is typically something which accompanies another activity, like watching television or a DVD, and even if everyone is at home they may be in separate rooms eating different meals. If a child is a particularly fussy eater parents may even have encouraged this behaviour rather than face a nightly tantrum over the table after a hard day's work.

Reinstating the family meal

Does this scenario sound frighteningly familiar to your own family's eating patterns? If it does, it's time to reclaim the family dining table and insist that everyone sits down to eat together at least three or four times a week. It can affect not just your family relationships but also your child's health and well-being in ways you might not have thought possible.

Your child may not easily give up her disorganized eating habits, in which case you will have to do some work at selling the idea of having regular family meals again. If she has got used to always eating dinner on a tray in her bedroom or while watching her favourite programme she will probably get very resentful if she is asked to turn it off and come to the table. She will have to be convinced that it is far more pleasant to be eating with the whole family than hunched in front of the television with a plate on her knee.

Some coercion on your part may be necessary to prevent this behaviour but try gentle persuasion at first. The last thing you want to do is to turn mealtimes into a battlefield as that will only diminish the mutual pleasure it should bring you all. Suggesting that she invites a friend to dinner from time to time may help her to be a little more enthusiastic.

Set the table as attractively as possible, with nice linen and cutlery. Your child can be involved in this – it's a task even pre-schoolers can manage without too much help. Fresh flowers and candles can make it seem more of an occasion, too. Make sure there is a jug of water or fruit juice to hand so that your child will be less tempted to demand a fizzy drink with her meal. Most importantly, turn off the television, radio or the CD player and talk!

Of course, the family meal doesn't necessarily have to be at the dining table. On sunny summer evenings what is nicer than eating in the garden or taking a picnic to the park? The important thing is that it is something you are doing together.

Neither does the shared meal have to be a three-course effort; it might be a simple supper of soup and bread and cheese, and there is nothing wrong with the occasional takeaway as long as you are all sharing it. However, establishing this new routine should make you feel much more enthusiastic about the types of meals you prepare and can also provide an opportunity to demonstrate your own healthy eating habits to your child. Perhaps you find it difficult to be creative about the type of meals you offer but with a little forward planning you should be able to draw up a menu for the week, which will help you create a healthy, balanced family diet. It's important to involve your child in the planning by encouraging her to help with the shopping and cooking. Children are often much keener to eat meals they have helped prepare themselves.

There is no doubt of the benefits of establishing regular family meals. It isn't just the routine of sitting down to dinner as a family, it is also the structure and atmosphere of family meals which can have such positive effects. Research carried out in the USA showed that young people, especially adolescent girls, were much less likely to develop eating disorders or to obsess about their weight if they regularly enjoyed eating with their families. They were also much more likely to eat fruit and vegetables rather than snack on junk food and were also less likely to become smokers or heavy drinkers.

Structured meal times help to give children a sense of security. Young children enjoy their predictability and they also offer every member of the family a much needed opportunity to interact with each other. There used to be a saying, 'The family that prays together stays together.' 'The family that eats together stays together' might be just as appropriate at the beginning of the twenty-first century.

The family meal can help keep the lines of communication open, even with a recalcitrant teenager. Take care to keep the atmosphere as convivial as possible. Resist the temptation to talk about work with your partner, something from which the child will almost inevitably be excluded. Try instead to keep to topics which involve the whole family and on which everyone can have an opinion. Be careful to keep the conversation positive and friendly. This is not the time to tackle the issues of untidy bedrooms or poor exam results!

The family meal gives parents the opportunity to demonstrate their own healthy eating habits, although this definitely doesn't mean regaling the family with details of the latest diet, a word which should be strictly banned at the dinner table.

It also gives you the opportunity to re-educate your child if she has fallen into bad habits or does not behave properly at the table. It's essential that she learns some basic etiquette, such as using the right cutlery or helping to serve other members of the family before herself. Such habits will stand her in very good stead when she reaches adulthood.

If your child tends to pile her plate high you can send out subtle messages about portion control. Talk about feeling full and not necessarily having to finish everything on her plate. Never force your child to eat up everything on her plate or she will begin to lose the ability to know when she has had enough.

Self-image

Children are becoming more body conscious at a much earlier age; by the age of ten many girls are worried about becoming fat. Children as young as eight years may be constantly hopping on the bathroom scales or talking about going on a diet. They have learnt from a very early age that being a certain shape and size is desirable and will make them feel more attractive and popular. The problem can be exacerbated when a girl reaches puberty and begins to panic at the way her body is becoming more shapely. For some girls this panic persists, and then eating disorders are likely to develop. She finds it impossible to accept that some simple adjustments to her lifestyle, such as sensible eating and regular exercise, are all she needs.

Modern day society and the cult of celebrity has made us transfixed by physical appearance and young people, particularly girls, are confronted daily with images of perfect faces and bodies to which they feel they should aspire. It seems to them that they can only be successful and happy if they are as slim and beautiful as the famous models and film stars they see constantly in magazines and on the screen.

The problem is that these images are not honest ones; your

child is being deceived. If one does meet a celebrity, who is noted for her perfect skin, hair and body, it can come as a surprise that in the flesh she looks much like anyone else. We see celebrities mainly either in photographs, in which every skin blemish has been airbrushed out and facial features technically enhanced, or on the screen when they have had the attention of a whole army of make-up artists and hairdressers – and, possibly, a plastic surgeon or two! Suggesting to girls that they should aim for this level of perfection is simply dishonest.

Young boys are not immune from this type of propaganda but the images to which they are encouraged to aspire tend to be athletic and sporty and are, therefore, a little more realistic.

Body shapes go in and out of fashion and what is considered desirable now may not be the same in another ten years. A couple of generations ago the ideal female body was the opposite of what it is today. Shapeliness was considered a sign of beauty and good health and Marilyn Monroe with her size 16 figure was the ideal. The thin outline we strive for today was once considered sickly and unattractive. However, since the 1960s the slender, narrow-hipped frame of the model has been seen as the peak of attractiveness. The fashionable body for the early twenty-first century is very slim but with full breasts, rather like a Barbie doll, an almost impossible combination for most women to achieve.

In past times women were able to change the shape of their bodies according to what was fashionable, with the help of constricting underwear like tight corsets and girdles. Now that the current fashion is for rather minimal clothing such as cropped tops and tiny miniskirts, there is nowhere to hide corsetry and the slightest bulge is inevitably on show. No wonder young girls become unhappy with the way they look and why, with such strong pressure, many of them turn to unhealthy ways of controlling their weight. From research carried out on a group of women in the USA, the unfortunate news appears to be that those who try the hardest to lose weight as adolescents are the most likely to become obese adults. The link has not yet been clearly defined but the suggestion is that early dieting may disrupt the metabolism of teenage girls, setting them up for obesity later in life.

The study further showed that women who started dieting before the age of 14 were far more likely to be constantly on diets than women who began dieting later. More than half of those who had dieted from the age of 14 said they were never able to maintain a permanent weight loss.

We are beginning to understand that dieting can actually lead to weight gain. It is now believed that severe restriction of calories forces the metabolism to lose less energy as heat and use more for fuelling the body.

Rather as we have developed a taste for instant food, we also seem to want instant diets – those which we hope will help us to lose a large amount of weight in the shortest possible time. A whole industry has been built upon the promise that this is possible. However, a rapid weight loss cannot normally be sustained. Help your child to accept that she can only lose a significant amount of weight very slowly and that, if this is necessary, it should be done with balanced eating and exercise.

Striving for some impossible ideal, obsessively weighing herself and counting calories is no way to enjoy her childhood and adolescence. Instead, your child should be encouraged to aim for more realistic goals, a healthy, fit body which works superbly, and an interesting, well-rounded personality. Self-obsession is never attractive and overweight can be a state of mind as well as of body.

Is your child being bullied?

An overweight child is quite likely to be bullied by his peers. Children are bullied for all sorts of reasons, whether it be for having protruding ears or ginger hair, but children who are fat are very obvious targets.

Bullying is an ongoing and age-old problem but should never be taken lightly. A child who is badly bullied at school may never truly recover and may indeed become severely depressed or even suicidal.

The victim of bullying tends to be a quiet, passive child who often finds it difficult to make friends. He does not usually retaliate because he doesn't have the physical or verbal skills to do so. The overweight child is at a particular disadvantage as he may not be able to run around with the other children in the playground or take part in organized games. The consequence is that he is left alone, looking vulnerable, on the sidelines – an obvious target for the class bully. Teachers may also be unsympathetic to the overweight child, who they may think of as being lazy or slow.

Boys are more likely to be physically bullied than girls; girls often suffer non-violent, more subtle harassment in the form of being dropped by a group of friends or having rumours spread about them. However, bullying can take many forms. It can involve name-calling, extortion, or stealing or damaging the victim's property. With the advent of mobile phones and e-mails bullying has been given new dimensions – the child cannot escape the torment even when at home.

Some children endure this kind of terrorism day after day. Imagine how it must feel to go to school knowing that the bullies are lying in wait for you, to call you names, tease, torment and humiliate you. What must that do for a child's self-esteem? How can he possibly be expected to thrive in that type of environment?

Never ignore your suspicions that your child may be being bullied, even if he refuses to talk about it himself. Often this is because he feels ashamed of what is happening to him, so it is up to you to recognize the signs and take action immediately. The most obvious indicators that something is going badly wrong are:

- Your child seems fearful about going to school.
- He regularly complains about feeling ill on school days.
- Items of clothing or school equipment go missing on a regular basis.
- His clothes and books are ripped and dirty.
- He appears to have few friends.

You must inform the school of your suspicions as soon as possible, even if your child insists that there is nothing wrong. Some schools are very sensitive to the issues of bullying and have a well-thought-out anti-bullying policy which can be very effective in reducing the incidence of bullying. Other schools tend to deny that it is happening, but it is precisely in those schools which boast that they have no bullying that the most serious cases are likely to occur.

It's true that you will find bullying to some degree in every school, but a good school is proactive in their approach and deals with it promptly and fairly, while a bad school wants to just sweep it under the carpet. Even when an anti-bullying policy is in place a poor school will pay only lip-service to it rather than make a real effort to counteract the behaviour.

You should try to get hold of a copy of the school's anti-bullying policy and talk to the class teacher or the teacher responsible for your child's pastoral care. If you have no joy there go straight to the head teacher. If the head dismisses your concerns you can approach the governing body. Start with a parent governor whose role it is to be the link between parents and school staff. Be persistent; your child has the right to be safe and happy in school.

You owe it to your child to stop the bullying. Don't ever say to him that he needs to stand up for himself or that he should ignore the taunts. Even adults find it difficult to stand up to an onslaught of bullying in the workplace, so why should we expect a child, particularly one who has little self-confidence, to do so?

If the school refuses to co-operate or simply seems unable

to deal with the problem, you may have to consider sending your child to another school where bullying is dealt with more severely.

It is heartbreaking to know that your child is being bullied; but it can be very alarming to discover that your child is the one doing the bullying. Persistent bullies usually come from homes where physical and/or verbal violence is a regular occurrence, but sometimes a child from an apparently caring, well-ordered home can start hitting or name-calling other children. Often this is a sign that he is under some kind of stress. Younger children who are experiencing a family break-up or bereavement find it difficult to express their feelings and sometimes show their anger by being unkind to other children. Children who are very bright often alleviate boredom at school by using wit or sarcasm to humiliate or sideline other children. Boys and girls who are tall or well-built may use their strength to intimidate others.

Sometimes it is an indication that your child is watching too many violent television programmes or films – including cartoons – or playing inappropriate computer games, so you need to be extra vigilant. A sudden increase in aggressive behaviour may also indicate that he is mixing with a new group of friends where bullying and intimidation of other children is acceptable.

Whatever the cause, you must make your disapproval and disappointment clear to him and seek professional help to try to get to the root of the problem if he persists in such unpleasant behaviour.

4

Creating an invisible fitness programme

It is a fact that most children walk less than their parents did at their age and considerably less than their grandparents would have done as children. As already discussed, many children are ferried by car to and from school, either because parents simply don't have the time to walk them there due to the demands of their jobs, or because the school is no longer automatically situated close to their home. After-school activities create more deadlines and further use of the car. In addition to this major lifestyle change, children are enticed into spending longer and longer in front of the TV, watching programmes that are specifically aimed at them, and/or playing the latest computer game, which they then go on to discuss at length on the phone with friends who may live on the other side of town. This is a far cry from the days when children spent most of their free time playing outside in the streets or parks where they lived, with friends who were usually also their next-door neighbours. And while we may want to campaign for safer streets and more play areas, we also need to address the issue of our children's fitness with the situation as it exists at present.

Very young children are almost always happy to join in with whatever physical activity you suggest to them, unless they are feeling ill, but once children reach school age the story starts to change. Going for a walk specifically because it is raining so that you can jump in the puddles starts to appeal more to parents, especially those who have been stuck in front of a computer for most of the day, than to children who sense that it is more sophisticated to stay indoors and hug the remote control.

Children who have been in school all day consider that they have completed a day's work and once they get in the habit of rushing home to a snack and their favourite programmes they will feel very hard done by if you try to insist they need fresh air and exercise. If your child is at the infant stage then it may well be that she runs around playing 'chase' every break and lunchtime, but children at junior stage seem to spend more time in chess and computer clubs, or even finishing off class work, during their breaktimes than they do in free play and exercise. In addition to this, if your child is already slightly or moderately overweight, he is a lot less likely to join in with physical activity, be it in PE lessons, in the playground or with the rest of his family. Even being slightly overweight will slow a child down, sap his energy and make it more difficult for him to keep up with his peers, and once this starts to happen he will become demoralized and give up trying.

There are two ways to counteract all of the above, assuming that you do not intend to sell the family car and set up a commune of like-minded people. The first method is to set about finding one or more sports or activities that your child can enjoy and that he will stick with. The second way is to create an invisible fitness programme that gets results but which your child or children are virtually unaware of. Ideally, you will be able to involve your child in both methods.

Sports and activities

Before discussing specific sports and activities there are a few points worth mentioning that are guaranteed to help you beat your child's resistance to getting fit:

1 You must join in. Obviously you don't need to don a football jersey and rush at the goalie, especially if the child in goal is only ten years old; but setting an example is key where children are concerned. It simply won't work if you flop down on the sofa with a packet of crisps when you arrive home from work but expect your child to get outside and kick a ball or play tennis.

30

2 If you always hated PE at school and have no interest at all in physical fitness you must keep this sad fact to yourself. Right now you must put on a convincing act for the sake of your child and try to find a relative or close friend who loves playing badminton, swimming or running and who would be willing to share her enthusiasm with you and your child.

3 You must never, ever force your child to embark on an activity or sport that he has no interest in, or compare him to sporty, active friends.

4 Without making a huge announcement or seeking confrontation, reduce the number of TV channels you opt for or drop cable altogether, and organize mealtimes and homework periods so that there is adequate time in your family schedule for physical activity.

A child who is unwilling to engage in physical activity is unlikely to respond with any enthusiasm to the after-school clubs and junior gym type classes that are widely available. While it may seem to you to be the ideal solution to the problem, because all you have to do is sign the form and write the cheque, you will almost certainly be wasting your money and everyone's time. Resist the urge to respond to every school letter that is brought home or flyer that comes through the letterbox. If your child expresses an interest in learning to fence or taking up judo you can afford to show a degree of casual enthusiasm, but you should not expect an overnight change in the level of fitness achieved, or even that the course will be completed. Also, if and when your child decides that a particular activity is not for him or that he 'can't do it', try not to react by showing your frustration or pointing out to him how much it has cost you, because next time he is less likely to want to try at all.

There are several ways in which you can tempt an unwilling child to get moving. Not surprisingly, if you love playing badminton or swimming and exercise regularly, your child is more likely to accept the activity as something he will want to try. This may mean sacrificing some of your own sessions in order to include your child in a way that will not be off-putting and that will provide some fitness benefits. For example, if tennis is your favourite activity, you are more likely to succeed in conveying how much fun it is if you introduce your child to the sport in a casual manner rather than by demonstrating how skilful you are and how easily you can thrash your little one. Making your child run around after the balls you've smashed across the net may get her running in the short term but she is unlikely to want to learn to play the game. Hiring a court for half an hour and inviting one or two of your child's friends to join in is likely to produce a lot more willing running around and is much more fun. Don't feel that you have to pay for coaching unless your child asks for it, but if he starts to really show an interest you could investigate local classes and clubs. In the beginning, stick to one or two sessions a month and try other activities at the same time, so that your child's fitness gradually improves enough to enable him to play his chosen game, but there is no pressure on him to become a sports star. Remember, if your encouragement reeks of desperation your child will feel pressurized and is more likely to back away.

Another, rather surprising, way of enticing your child towards sport is via her favourite computer games, TV programmes and films. Next time your child is plugged in to the PlayStation, take a long look at the character she is operating with the game controller. In most cases the object of her attention will be an athletic, death-defying creature who executes the most amazing (and impossible) physical moves. You can make your move by pointing out that much of what is happening on screen is based on tae kwon do and other martial arts. Tae kwon do, judo and karate all provide an excellent means of becoming fit and if you take your child along to your local club it is highly likely that she will come away impressed by what she has seen. Most martial arts clubs have a junior section and/or sessions where you can see everyone from eight to 80 having a go. Martial arts classes are particularly suited to children because they are run in a disciplined way, with a set routine of warming up, sometimes with games like tag and chase, and stretching exercises, followed by a teaching period of the set moves and then practice with appropriate partners.

In tae kwon do, as in many other martial arts, the physical part is considered by its exponents to be a by-product of the art and its intrinsic philosophy, which lies in promoting characteristics within each individual of respect, courtesy, goodness, trustworthiness, self-control, loyalty, humility, courage, perseverance and patience. These attributes are to be gained through the physical practice, so your child will not be lectured on the philosophy, but you can put your mind at rest regarding any worries over the 'violent nature' of this type of exercise.

If your child loves animals and enjoys books and films about horses you could try introducing her to horse-riding. Many parents are deterred from trying this activity because of the expense and what they see as the inherent danger involved, but there are real fitness benefits to be gained. Regarding the expense, it is not necessary to arrange for lessons every single week, and many riding stables offer special days during school holidays when your child would have the chance to 'adopt' a pony and become involved in the care and management of a horse, as well as having an opportunity to ride, for not much more than the price of a single lesson. There is no need to purchase the full riding habit unless you are certain your child is to continue for the foreseeable future. Reputable riding stables lend out hats in good condition and with a chin strap, at no extra cost. Trainers or leather lace-ups (not Wellingtons) can be worn with track pants or leggings (not jeans, as they can rub). Once your child has learned how to do a rising trot she will expend considerable energy and horse-riding is a great boost to self-esteem and a sense of well-being.

The invisible fitness programme

An invisible fitness programme is something that you need to initiate and control to be of benefit to your child, without his resenting the routine or rebelling against what is going on. Acting in this way does not mean that you are setting out to deceive or manipulate your child: it simply means that you are quietly and gradually developing a family routine that will ensure everyone's good health.

Look first at your day-to-day routine and try to implement tiny changes that will not cause any worry to your child or major inconvenience to you. Remember, you are looking for a gradual improvement in your child's fitness, not an instant make-over. If you drive your child to school each day in the car, take the decision to park the car ten minutes' walk away and walk with him to the school gates. You can justify this change for several reasons: to counteract the difficult parking conditions near the school, a message from the school encouraging parents to walk with their children, or an honestly expressed desire on your part to get some air in the morning and chat to your child. Do not, on any account, tell your child you are instigating the short walk procedure because she is unfit or needs more exercise. You may be surprised how quickly your child learns to appreciate spending a little time with you before you both begin your working day and, providing you can make the sacrifice of getting up a little earlier in the mornings, you can gradually extend the walk. The key here is to take things very gradually and allow your child to adjust to the new routine before you rush to change things again. If your child thinks you are going to keep 'upping the ante' she is likely to rebel.

Look at how your family life works and try to find other opportunities when short walks can be slipped into the routine without your child resenting it. Perhaps your child enjoys a regular comic or magazine, which you could both walk to the shop to buy and maybe incorporate into a longer browsing outing through other shops. Cancel newspaper/

magazine deliveries and subscriptions so that you have to go out.

Even if you have never been an outdoor kind of a family, you could start by arranging a picnic and include a ball or Frisbee in with your supplies, to play with before or after the meal. Once you have managed to get children outside and away from the TV and computer, half the battle is won and they are likely to be more willing to move around and take some exercise.

Clever combining of outings will also help build up a child's fitness. For example, if you are taking your child to the cinema you could choose a complex that also has a skating rink, bowling alley or climbing wall close by. Allow time before the film to take a look at these activities and before you know it you'll be skating around together.

Make the most of your child's interests and enthusiasms. If you have a garden it is imperative that family activities are included in the design. Rose gardens and water features can come when the children grow up – while they are young you should make space for impromptu ball games, a basket ball hoop, table tennis, badminton – whatever you can squeeze in. If the equipment is there children will use it, provided you spend time in the garden as well. If you are a keen gardener you will have to restrict yourself to tough plants that can survive rough treatment and ignore the trampled-on lawn.

When you plan family outings make sure there will be opportunity for walking, climbing or bicycling – a child who is interested in castles and history in general will not object to climbing hills to get to some – and consider holidays that you know will include plenty of physical activity. Holidays are an ideal time to introduce activities that your child may not have had the confidence to attempt at home. Messing about with boats on holiday could lead to a canoeing course once your child gets back home, providing you manage to stay enthusiastic without being overly pushy.

There will inevitably be times when the weather, your child's mood and your own inclinations combine to keep everyone indoors. However, this should not be seen as a break from your fitness programme and you should not allow your child to slip back into old habits or you will have to start all over again. Aerobics and fitness routine DVDs can be bought very cheaply or borrowed from your local library, and once you've pushed the furniture out of the way this is something you can easily do indoors. With young children you will need to view the DVD first on your own to ensure that it does not demonstrate anything too difficult or inappropriate. At the very least your child and yourself are bound to laugh together when you start to copy the moves on the tape. Once you have got the general gist of a musical routine you may prefer just to play your child's favourite songs and jump around for ten minutes together. All you have to do is wear loose clothing and make sure your child does the same. Have a blanket ready for any floor work you are going to attempt and wear trainers if you are going to do lots of jumping up and down. Dance mats with accompanying instruction DVDs and music also help to get children moving and tune in to their desire to watch a screen at the same time.

A mini trampoline or rebounder is another inexpensive prop that can be pushed under a bed or behind a cupboard when not in use. The benefits of rebounding have been researched and endorsed by the American space agency, NASA, and in addition to the obvious benefit of increasing fitness, there is anecdotal evidence that rebounding can help with conditions as varied as asthma and hyperactivity. No special clothing is required and the exercise is done barefoot. Your child is likely to enjoy rebounding to music or even in front of her favourite cartoon and to begin with a two or three minute 'work-out' will be sufficient. Rebounders come with a set of instructions for varying the exercise you do and there is also a selection of books published on the subject. If you have space to leave the rebounder where it can be seen without being an obstruction then your child is more likely to jump on and have a go when she is passing by.

Exercise can also be literally incorporated into everyday living. Don't keep the housework all to yourself – involve your child at a physical level – you'll be preparing him for life in more ways than one. If you have floors that need polishing, tie dusters to your child's feet, put on some music and let him dance the floor clean. Window cleaning, dusting and mopping can all be done energetically and to music to help your child burn off some calories. The key to mundane activity is to set an example, be positive and make it fun.

5

Avoiding pushy parent syndrome, introducing non-competitive activities, puppy fat, 'fat camps'

Almost all parents are guilty of being 'pushy' at one time or another, simply because they care so much about their child's well-being. However, it is a trap you should beware of falling into, simply because you will end up doing more harm than good. The temptation, when we see our children gaining weight and becoming lethargic, or missing out on opportunities we know they would enjoy in order to watch TV instead, is to step in and, metaphorically, give them a shove in the right direction.

Encourage, don't push

Perhaps you've gone along to a school football match and noticed the parents on the sidelines, shouting advice and picking their children out for individual coaching while they are actually trying to play the game? Have you ever talked to another parent who takes her child's swimming certificates as seriously as if they were an honours degree, or enrols her child in ballet classes because she herself never had the chance as a child or, worse still, gave up and wished she hadn't? Slimming clubs are full of adults who played plenty of sport as children, but stopped the moment they could possibly do so. Being forced, or bribed, to take part in a sport or class that you did not choose to embark on yourself is the best way of being put off physical activity for the rest of your life. This is why adults talk about their old PE teachers and games lessons more frequently than about any other school subject; because being forced to run, jump, climb ropes or vault over a wooden horse when you have no desire and perhaps no ability to do so is unforgettable in the worst kind of way. So, the next time you seize upon an advert for a junior sports club or make a note of a new tap dancing class you want to tell your child about, ask yourself if she has ever expressed the slightest interest in playing that sport or going to dance classes.

Children are sensitive to the feelings of others, especially their parents. If you frequently suggest new forms of activity your child could embark upon she will quickly begin to understand your underlying message that she needs to get fitter. She will feel that you are not satisfied with her the way she is, that she is, in your eyes, not the kind of child that you would wish to have or who reaches your high standards. The natural reaction to this kind of insidious and underlying criticism is to try to switch off in order to avoid being hurt. Even if your child attempts to do what you suggest her heart is unlikely to be in it, and when she fails she is going to feel worse and is unlikely to want to try again.

Do not confuse adopting a pushy attitude with a healthy interest in your child's activities. If your child wants to try a new sport or class, then by all means encourage him by paying for the tuition, buying the kit and asking how it's going. That's how far parental encouragement should go! You do not need to observe every class, scream from the sidelines, give advice on where she's going wrong, or comment on fellow team members or classmates. There should be no discussion with other parents on the activity except to say 'it seems like they're having fun', and there should certainly be no after-class chats with the teacher to discover if your child has 'talent' or if she might benefit from extra classes. The urge to relive your childhood and/or improve on it, through your child, should be resisted at all costs: it is of no benefit to your child whatsoever. Similarly, if you are a super-fit badminton player or swimmer, it does not automatically follow that your child will share your enthusiasm and, while it's permissible to introduce your child to the sport in a low-key way if he expresses an interest, it is unforgivable to force participation because you 'know it will do him good'.

If you know yourself to be less than fit there is a temptation to resort humbly to the ploy of 'I don't want you to grow up like me, son', especially if you weren't given the chance as a child to try out sports you might have enjoyed; but this seemingly genuine concern is simply another way of burdening your child with the responsibility of taking part in something that is of your choosing and from your motivation rather than his own. If you are genuinely concerned that your own lack of fitness might influence your child adversely, then you should think about setting a different kind of example. Your child is more likely to want to try a new sport or activity if you take up something that is new to you both and quietly persevere with it.

Non-competitive activities

What puts many children off sport is that ultimately it is competitive. Nobody enjoys losing, and losing on a regular basis can be totally demoralizing. It is possible, when playing a team game, to become effective at 'hiding' within the team and to allow your team-mates to support you with their efforts so that your weakness or lack of talent does not hinder the game's progress. However, most children would not actively seek to play under such conditions and would definitely not choose to play, for fun, a sport they felt themselves to be weak at. Do not be fooled by the old-fashioned concept that it will do your child good to learn to lose on the sports field or that it will toughen him up to play a game he detests. Losing at games is not a preparation for life. If a child loves playing a certain sport he will not mind losing games, because he wants to play again in order to win and losing will help to motivate him to play harder next time. However, if a child dislikes sport, he will not become convinced to play it for pleasure simply because his team wins or loses. Schools have been criticized for being too competitive on the sports field and have tried to combat this in many instances by playing diluted versions of certain games and by having co-operative sports days. This kind of activity has met with limited success and is not, on the whole, appealing to most children. Similarly, if you seek to encourage your child to play a game that is designed to be played in a competitive manner in a neutral or non-competitive way, you are unlikely to enthuse her or help her to get fit because the game will not produce the kind of energy and output that is expended when it is played competitively.

T'ai chi

Naturally non-competitive activities are likely to be of interest and to meet with more success with children who dislike competing. T'ai chi, for example, aims to promote graceful, dance-like movements that increase self-awareness, co-ordination and balance. The practice includes 37 basic postures and around 128 complete movements. As the postures are learnt they are linked together to form sequences of movements. Some of the reported benefits of t'ai chi are better breathing and relaxation, improved circulation and improved all-round fitness and well-being. T'ai chi is very much aimed at a gradual acquiring of skills and learning of the postures. Classes repeat basic postures and then add to them each time, so that children can benefit from a set routine and enjoy adding to their repertoire. There is no singling-out pupils for criticism, and the only kit that is required is loose, comfortable clothing, so it is unlikely that your child would ever feel self-conscious or embarrassed in this environment. Some schools have begun to introduce t'ai chi into PE and Movement classes and reports of benefits in terms of increased concentration and self-esteem are very encouraging. There is no upper or lower age limit to participating in this activity.

Yoga

Yoga is a vast discipline with many branches and types of practice. Children usually respond best when they are introduced to the physical aspects of yoga, so look out for Iyengar classes. These classes include a great number of postures, varying from the easy to the very difficult according to pupils' experience, and breathing techniques are taught to complement the postures. Yoga is said to bring about a sense of inner calm when it is practised regularly and, again, teachers report results as varied as increased self-esteem and more self-control among pupils who have been taught yoga within schools. As with t'ai chi, there is no lower or upper age limit for practising yoga, and loose clothing, bare feet and a non-slip mat are the only equipment requirements.

Korfball

While, strictly speaking, korfball does not fall into the 'non-competitive' category it most definitely is a sport worth trying for children who feel intimidated by the aggressive tackling and fouling indigenous to football and rugby. Korfball is the fastest growing sport in Europe and it's the only sport that is intended to be played with mixed gender teams and co-operative manoeuvres. In a game of korfball everyone gets the chance to defend and attack because everyone swaps ends and positions. Girls are not positioned directly against boys but form an equal part of the team of eight. Most games last around 15 minutes only so korfball is an ideal way of increasing fitness without exhausting and demoralizing a less than confident child. The rules of korfball also ensure that there is no rough play and are designed to encourage healthy interaction between the sexes. Korfball is frequently described as a cross between netball and basketball, but as players are not allowed to run with the ball there is no physical contact and the superstar element of the individual very tall and athletic player is eliminated.

Puppy fat

'Puppy fat' is a term that is bandied about to describe almost every developmental stage from babyhood onwards. Perhaps the most common use of this term, though, is in connection with children approaching puberty who (hopefully) go on to lose their excess weight as they grow taller with age. Puppy fat frequently coincides with children doing less activity as they become more self-conscious – they are less likely to race around burning off excess calories. Girls seem to be labelled in this way more frequently than boys, as they develop fuller figures. Whatever the context in which this term is used it is not at all helpful or necessary. Labelling a child as having puppy fat does two things. First, it provides the child and the parent with a bland and vague excuse for why the child is overweight and postpones the day when the issue of their overweight and lack of fitness must be addressed. Second, whether the prefix is 'puppy', 'kitten' or any other seemingly innocuous word, it is still attached to the unpleasant description 'fat', which is likely to be demoralizing and self-fulfilling for the child. Banish the phrase from your vocabulary and discourage others from using it in connection with your child.

Sometimes parents use terms like 'puppy fat' to try and make the idea of their child being less than 'perfect' more acceptable in their own eyes. Looking for excuses and reasons why your child is overweight and trying to justify how they look can mask parental guilt about the fact that you find your child less appealing now than when she was a toddler or baby. All parents want to be proud of their children and we are all conditioned by the media to value beauty and good looks. If you are slim and fit yourself you are more likely to feel that your child is letting the family down when you grab hold of that roll of fat as you cuddle him. You will most certainly feel terribly guilty as well, for having such 'hard-hearted' thoughts about your own child. However, do not confuse a temporary distaste or dislike of your child's appearance with feeling a lack of love for her.

The two things are entirely separate. The key lies in channelling any thoughts of distaste for your child's physique into a positive desire to help him become fit and healthy, without letting him know about either your guilty thoughts or your helpful plans.

When to seek medical advice

When a child is between 20 and 25 per cent heavier than their ideal weight for height they may be considered to be 'obese' by their doctor or health visitor. However, unless your doctor has mentioned overweight as a contributory factor to another condition that is troubling your child, such as asthma, you may still prefer to tackle the problem as a family using some or all of the suggestions in this book.

If you decide to address your child's weight problem without consulting your GP you must be very wary indeed of putting your child on a diet. A lack of calcium in the diet during childhood and adolescence can lead to osteoporosis later in life; it should be remembered that 90 per cent of bone mass is laid down between the ages of 13 and 17. Similarly, a low iron intake in the diet can cause anaemia, with its attendant problems of fatigue, irritability and weakness. Most important of all, putting your child on a diet now may condemn her to a lifetime of dieting and a negative attitude towards food.

However, if you have been trying unsuccessfully for some time to provide a healthy and balanced diet for your child and to see that she gets a moderate amount of exercise each day, but feel you are getting nowhere, while your child continues to gain weight and feel unhappy, you should definitely consult your GP. In circumstances where your child openly expresses his concern and is obviously very overweight you can afford to adopt a down-to-earth approach as you would with any other ailment, while retaining your commitment to helping the whole family to stick to a healthy lifestyle.

Your GP may refer you and your child to a nutritionist or she may recommend a weight maintenance programme herself. Resist the urge to use the 'diet' word in connection with your child's treatment and do not encourage family talk along the lines of what your child may or may not be allowed to eat. The eating programme that your child will be asked to follow will be a 'maintenance' programme rather than a weight reduction programme, with the intention of allowing your child's weight to be caught up by his height as he grows older. With programmes like this it takes 18 months for every 20 per cent excess weight your child is carrying, before your child reaches his 'ideal' weight/height ratio.

The biggest part you will play at this point is helping your child to keep motivated. Eighteen months is a long time in a child's life, and these days most of us are used to expecting instant results, but this is definitely the safest and most effective way of tackling serious overweight in children. Once your child is prescribed an eating programme she will be regularly monitored in sessions with the nutritionist where you and she will have the chance to discuss problems and ideas. If your child has reached the stage where he is desperate to do something about his weight then he is likely to welcome the chance of formalizing things and you should retain a positive outlook for the future and provide him with all the moral support he needs.

'Fat camps'

So-called 'fat camps' are a phenomenon of the USA but they are gradually beginning to appear in this country. The first thing to mention is that the term itself is not one that any of the proponents of these camps would use about themselves and it is certainly not a term that is likely to appeal to children.

Opponents of this type of camp maintain that it is tantamount to punishment and imprisonment to send a child away because she is overweight, and that it will inevitably lead to the child having poor self-esteem. However, being severely overweight is also likely to lead to a child having poor self-esteem. Camps that have been set up in this country, unlike their US counterparts, only admit children who are obese according to the World Health Organization guidelines, and not simply those whose parents think they need to lose weight and change their shape and image.

Also, in contrast to US examples, camps in the UK do not seek to reduce their participants' calorie intake to drastically low levels – they do not set out to bring about weight loss, but aim instead for the children to gain muscle density and lose fat through exercise and moderating their eating habits. The average weight of a child attending a fitness camp in this country is around 13 stone but some may weigh as much as 20 stone. Most children stay at a camp for between a fortnight and six weeks, during which time they are encouraged to participate in cookery and nutrition classes, as well as try new sports and activities and discuss any issues or problems they may have relating to their weight.

Obviously, this type of camp is expensive (around £2,000 for a six-week stay), although some local councils are prepared to help fund places in extreme circumstances. The most important criterion if you are considering a 'fat camp' for your child is to ensure, absolutely and completely, that she would not view the experience as having a stigma attached to it. Unless you and your child view the idea of going to a camp in an entirely positive light there is simply no point in proceeding. As far as your child is concerned you need to be 100 per cent sure that she will not see the camp as a punishment and not feel she has failed you in some way.

You need to be certain that your child is mature enough to be happy being away from home for more than a few days at a time. Twelve years old is normally the youngest age at which children attend camps in the UK. You also need to impress upon him, without applying undue pressure, that going to the camp means making a firm commitment to carrying through the advice and activities that are embarked upon there.

As far as you are concerned, you have to be sure that you can afford financially and emotionally to let your child go. If the financial burden is such that you would resent it if your child returned and remained overweight, or it was clear that the experience had not worked for him, then you should forget the idea completely. If you know you will end up feeling guilty at sending your child away for someone else to deal with, and that you will feel a failure at having to resort to this, then it would also be in your family's best interests if you turned your attention to other remedies.

6

The onset of puberty, eating disorders

Once your child reaches the teenage years it becomes even more difficult to monitor what he is eating. He is now, inevitably, beginning to develop a life independent of you and this could mean that he will rebel against the eating habits instilled by his family and begin to opt for fast food and takeaway meals instead. Your child is likely to be approaching the reckless stage so common in adolescence when teenagers simply refuse to worry about the future and what will happen to them if they don't look after themselves. That's why many children of this age begin to experiment with smoking, drinking and even illegal drugs and seem not to care too much about their daily nutritional needs.

The occasional burger or doner kebab is not going to do too much harm. One reason why so many young people tend to eat this type of food is that there are very few places where young teenagers can meet together, and hamburger bars and pizza parlours act as social centres. As a parent you also have to compete with massive advertising campaigns from the major fast food outlets aimed directly at your child.

As long as he is continuing to eat the nutritious, well-balanced meals you provide when he is at home there is no serious cause for concern, but try to make him aware that an optimal level of fitness will help him cope better, both physically and emotionally, with all the changes he is currently undergoing.

The growth spurts and changing body shape can make it more difficult for you to assess whether your child is as fit and healthy as he should be. He is probably now, as is quite normal, insisting on a new level of privacy and won't let you see him undressed so it can be difficult to know whether or not he is putting on too much weight.

Some children go through puberty with no problems at all,

but others find it very difficult to cope with their changing shape and the obvious signs that they are leaving their childhood behind for the frightening grown-up world. It is those children who are at much more risk of eating disorders, as will be discussed later.

Has puberty begun?

Puberty is occurring much earlier – 11 to 12 years is now normal – and it is easy to recognize that your child has reached this stage in her life. Most girls have a growth spurt around the age of 11 (boys do not usually catch up for another two years or so; girls, initially, become taller and heavier than boys of a similar age). The first signs will be the enlargement of their nipples and the appearance of breast 'buds' and they will begin to gain height and weight very quickly. The next stage is usually the appearance of pubic and underarm hair, although in some girls this may happen earlier. Breasts will become fuller and hips widen. About a year later menstruation will begin, although periods do not normally start until around 17 per cent of body weight is laid down in fat, so very thin girls tend to start later.

The process in boys normally takes a little longer. Bones and muscles increase in size when the body begins producing the hormone testosterone. The most obvious changes include the broadening of the shoulders and the enlargement of the testes, scrotum and penis, as well as facial and pubic hair. Some boys at the mid and late puberty stage have some breast tissue which can sometimes be the result of obesity but which, in most boys, usually regresses when full maturity is reached.

Some children, even those who have up until now been very slim, may begin to look a bit podgy around the time of puberty. They may be quite happy to discuss their worries about gaining weight with parents or friends but others may worry in secret and hide their burgeoning shape under baggy clothes.

A new, erratic eating pattern may be one reason why weight problems occur at this time. Your child, as we have already said, will probably be spending much more time out of the home and not joining you for every family meal. When he is in the house he may be staying in bed for longer and possibly skipping breakfast in the morning in order to get to school on time, and ending up with a bowl of cornflakes at three in the afternoon.

It is at this stage of their lives that some adolescents begin to develop eating disorders. If you have any suspicion that your child may be at risk you need to take action quickly and seek medical help. Disorders like anorexia and bulimia can have serious effects on the long-term health of your child and can, in extreme cases, be fatal.

Anorexia

Anorexia nervosa – 'appetite loss of nervous origins' – is often triggered in the early teenage years, although some girls as young as eight have been diagnosed. It is not the same as the loss of appetite which is the symptom of a physical illness or depression; rather it is specifically associated with fear of becoming fat. It is a condition which hardly exists in those countries where there is not enough food to go round and being plump is considered a sign of being wealthy. In contrast, in the West it is the poor who tend to be overweight and the wealthy, who can afford the best food and expensive gym membership and personal trainers, who are very thin.

Anorexia most commonly occurs in girls, but a small percentage of boys are also victims. Whereas most girls are of normal weight before they begin to cut back on food, male anorexics tend to start at above normal weight. Each person has different reasons and different circumstances for developing this eating disorder but it most usually begins when a young girl begins to worry obsessively about her weight. The concern may have been triggered by a chance remark from a relative, such as 'You're getting to be a big girl', or she may dislike her more curvaceous shape. She may be heavier than her sister or the least thin of her group of friends.

If your child is carrying a bit of extra weight you may be rather pleased if she begins to reduce her food intake or insists on going on a diet. Indeed you may even actively encourage her to cut back and as you see the weight drop off you will be pleased for her. Lots of compliments about her new appearance may give her self-confidence an initial boost and she may generally seem much happier; it is difficult to believe that her new eating patterns can be anything other than beneficial. However, although at the beginning her main aim was just to lose a few pounds, she may embark on a much more intensive – and ultimately destructive – form of dieting in order to see how far she can go. As her parent, you need to be aware of the warning signs that your child's preoccupation with her size and shape is definitely not healthy.

Research has indicated that the early onset of puberty can be linked with self-destructive behaviour. Sexual maturity is racing far ahead of emotional maturity and is leaving young teenagers confused and unhappy. One theory is that anorexia is an attempt to hold back the growing process and hang on to childhood. Indeed, one effect of anorexia is that it does halt the developing process. Confronted with impending adulthood and feeling unable to cope with the new pressures and demands this may bring, teenagers feel their lives are out of control. The one thing they are able to control is their food intake.

Is my child likely to become anorexic?

Although, as already discussed, eating disorders occur for a number of reasons, there are some characteristic traits which occur frequently in young people with anorexia. Sufferers are likely to be children who tend to be anxious and fearful. They often come from families where their parents seem to be supportive and loving but, in fact, may be over-controlling or have unrealistic expectations of what their child can achieve at school or college. Their teenager worries about failing and deep down may feel very resentful towards her parents. However, instead of expressing this by resorting to the more usual teenage rebellious behaviour – like staying out late or being insolent – she uses food as a method of punishing them. It is a way of establishing some degree of independence and giving her one means of control over the way she lives her life. Anorexia can also be triggered by problems at school, difficulty in making friends or being bullied.

There are some danger signals to look out for:

- The anorexic teenager expresses serious dissatisfaction with her body image and has a fear of being even a normal body weight.
- She seems to be toying with her food, pushing it around the plate, cutting it into small pieces and eating very slowly.
- She will eat the crusts of a sandwich but leave the centre part.
- She limits how much she drinks, believing that even water can make her fat.
- She is obsessed with weighing herself – perhaps several times a day – and she will worry about even the most minimal fluctuation.
- She always wears baggy clothes to cover up and hide her thinness.
- She may begin to exercise excessively and seems very knowledgeable about how many calories she has burned off.

As anorexia progresses you will notice that your child bruises easily and that she appears extra-sensitive to heat and cold. She will also become more susceptible to illnesses and may be plagued by coughs and colds. You may find her concentration is poor; she can't read a book or may even find

53

it difficult to take in what someone is saying to her. Other physical signs, although not outwardly obvious, are the loss of bone density and damage to the reproductive organs, which could leave her permanently infertile.

Anorexia is clearly a very serious condition which puts a tremendous strain on the whole family, including siblings, grandparents and beyond. It is unbelievably painful to watch someone you love so much deliberately inflicting severe harm on herself and risking her life. Family mealtimes become a battlefield and your child will respond badly to any attempts to help her, simply seeing you as someone who wants her to be fat.

Treatment must be sought and is most effective the earlier it begins, before the child has lost too much weight. The main problem is to convince someone suffering from anorexia that they do need help. A stay in hospital may be necessary in the more severe cases.

The treatment of anorexia is usually a holistic one, addressing your child's emotional and psychological needs as well as attending to her physical condition. Fortunately, the body can recover even after long periods of starvation once a healthy lifestyle is re-established.

Bulimia

Bulimia is, sadly, a very common condition in teenagers, although it does not take hold as early as anorexia and is more likely to occur in later adolescence. It may appear to be a completely different condition from anorexia, because far from refusing food, bulimiacs don't seem to be able to get enough to eat. Yet the conditions are very similar in that they both arise from a need to take control in some way and have similar underlying causes. As people with anorexia choose to ignore the signals that they are hungry, those with bulimia ignore the signals that they have eaten enough. It is possible to be both anorexic and bulimic as sufferers swing like a pendulum between the two conditions.

Bulimia, which translated means 'ox hunger', is much more common than was once thought and has only been recognized as a medical condition in the past 30 years. The sufferer is unable to stop eating even when she is feeling really full, but later, after the binge, in order to control her weight, she will make herself vomit or take laxatives. This pattern of behaviour is seen both in people who are over-weight and in those with anorexia who also have episodes of binge-eating.

Someone who is bulimic is also obsessed with her body size and shape and seems to be really fearful about gaining weight even if she is perfectly normal. Binge-eating is most likely to occur in people who have been seriously dieting for quite long periods and find that they crave food rich in sugar and fats, just the type of foods which someone concerned about their body weight should avoid. For a young person, dieting should never take the place of sensible eating and certainly a diet which involves diet pills or liquid food substitutes should never be followed, as these things are more likely to encourage bulimia.

People who develop bulimia often have very low self-esteem and are full of self-loathing and guilt about their behaviour, although they may appear on the surface to be very well-adjusted. That is why binge-eating is most often done in secret. Your suspicions should be aroused if you suddenly realize that food has been disappearing from the fridge on a regular basis without your knowledge, or if you find piles of chocolate or biscuit wrappers under your child's bed. Often the binges take place late at night when everyone else is asleep, which means she seems very tired the following morning.

Bulimia is often triggered by some crisis in the family – a divorce, a bereavement or even sexual abuse. However, there has been a trend in the past few years for celebrities to admit to bulimia – the late Princess of Wales, for example, and a number of models and actresses. While it is laudable that these problems are brought out into the open, some young girls want to emulate these people and for them binge-eating and then vomiting or taking laxatives may become acceptable behaviour. If you believe your child is part of a group for whom this is the norm you need to alert her to the risks she is taking with her health. It would also be wise to alert the parents of your child's friends so that you can make a concerted effort to put a stop to the behaviour. Laxatives can be very dangerous if taken on a regular basis. They cause irritation in the gastrointestinal tract and can permanently damage the lining of the bowel and prevent normal function. Constant vomiting makes the throat sore and inflamed and swallowing becomes painful. Bulimia may prove easier to treat than anorexia because sufferers are usually more prepared to acknowledge that they have an eating disorder. They need to learn to stop worrying excessively about their body shape and to resume a healthier pattern of eating. Often this can be done with the help of a psychologist or a counsellor but the love and understanding you give your child at this time will ultimately be the most effective way of returning her to good health.

Compulsive eating

Compulsive eating is similar in many ways to bulimia but it does not involve vomiting or taking laxatives. Many of us overeat from time to time as a form of comfort when we are upset about something, but the compulsive eater always eats more than she needs to. Not only does she eat large amounts but her intake will normally be heavily biased in favour of sugary, high-calorie foods. This, of course, results in swings in blood sugar levels, which will make her feel irritable and tired. A compulsive eater is often malnourished because of this overindulgence in sweet foods, rather than having a balanced diet.

Most people with compulsive eating disorder are obese and are therefore at risk of the many health problems we have already discussed. Overeating can start in childhood if parents themselves are overeaters and insist on pressing huge portions of food on their child as a misguided way of demonstrating their love. Inevitably this only helps to instil poor eating habits in the next generation. When parents are the cause of an eating disorder a child may only be able to break the pattern once she is away from home.

The compulsive eater will eat large amounts of food very frequently. She seems unable to control how much she eats and will eat much more quickly than is normal. As with other eating disorders, this compulsion is usually the result of some emotional upset or disappointment and eating is compensation for her unhappy feelings about herself. Counselling or therapy will probably be necessary to help her break the vicious circle.

7

Alienation, smoking, drinking, illegal drug-taking

Teenage obesity needs to be viewed within the wider context of overall health and lifestyle. Very few families get through adolescence without some kind of conflict; the reassuring news is that most survive and go on to form loving, close relationships with their children once they are through the difficult stage. However, some children do drive parents to their limits with their challenging behaviour. It is crucial to keep the lines of communication open at this stage even when you feel really infuriated and fed up, however rude and bad-tempered your child is. Even in the best-ordered families there will always be the occasional row when you have a teenager in the house.

If parents are not supportive and understanding at this time the teenager can become seriously alienated from the family, and then there is a much greater likelihood of their getting into trouble or taking risks with their health. This is the most likely time for them to begin smoking, drinking and experimenting with illegal drugs.

These dangers do not have class barriers. Middle-class, suburban children or those living in rural areas are just as much at risk, if not more so, from alcohol or drug abuse as the more stereotypical disaffected teenager living on an inner-city housing estate. In fact children with wealthy parents can find it easier to afford alcohol and drugs. The fact is that every parent needs to be aware of the dangers and to know what to do if they suspect their child is at risk. In order to counteract what is very dangerous behaviour you need, first, to arm yourself with all the facts so that you can offer calm, balanced arguments. A young person often assumes that his parents are ignorant about the use of illegal drugs, for example, and so won't spot the telltale signs, but equally he himself may be very misguided about what effect they will have on him. Making him aware of the risks he is running may help to give him ammunition when he is confronted by friends tempting him into undesirable behaviour. Many children try smoking, drinking or taking illegal substances simply out of curiosity but often do not understand how powerful the pull to keep on taking them can be and how easy it is to become addicted.

Smoking

Despite the fact that children probably learn at a young age about the dangers of smoking, many of them will begin to smoke regularly in their early teens – often because smoking curbs the appetite and they want to lose weight. Children are three times as likely to smoke if both parents smoke; parents' approval or disapproval can be a significant factor. Example is crucial and it is useless to preach to your child about smoking if he knows that you still indulge. Other children who don't witness smoking at home might have the occasional cigarette to show off to friends but don't get hooked in the same way. You and your partner must make sure that you have given up before lecturing your child. Do whatever you have to do to stop this life-threatening habit and if necessary enlist the help of your GP or one of the anti-smoking help groups.

Much has been done to try to discourage young people from smoking. There are bans on advertising, and education programmes in school set out the risks in graphic detail, as do anti-smoking television adverts. It is illegal to sell any tobacco product to anyone below the age of 16 and retailers can be heavily fined, yet a study carried out in 1996 estimated that £108 million received in tax came from the illegal sale of cigarettes to children!

Starting early is what most nicotine addicts have in common: 70 per cent of adult smokers had their first cigarette between the ages of 11 and 15. Advertising and particularly the sponsorship of sport by cigarette manufacturers all send out confusing messages to young people. There is some positive news in that the number of boys who smoke has decreased in recent years, but an increasing number of girls are taking up the habit. It's been estimated that one in five 15-year-old girls is a smoker. As mentioned above, one important factor seems to be that they believe smoking will help to keep them slim and are using cigarettes as an appetite suppressant. It isn't helpful when famous models and pop stars are photographed with a cigarette as it helps perpetuate the impression that smoking is cool and sophisticated. Peer pressure is also of great importance.

If your daughter smokes and refuses to heed warnings about future health problems, you may have more success if you stress how it can affect her appearance and will make her less attractive to the opposite sex. Knowing that smoking causes bad breath, stained teeth, a poor complexion and encourages cellulite will probably make more of an impression at this stage than if you regale her with statistics about the number of people who die prematurely from smoking-related illnesses. If your child is smoking in order to try to control her weight, ensure she understands the principles of healthy eating as laid out in this book and encourage her to take more exercise – a Christmas or birthday present of gym membership might be appropriate, for example.

If she remains defiant and insists that she should be free to indulge if she wishes, remind her that smoking, far from making her independent, will end in dependency on nicotine if she is not careful. Many young people are unaware just how addictive smoking can become and believe they will be able to stop whenever they want to. They need to know that it can be as difficult for smokers to kick the habit as it is for those who use heroin or cocaine.

The fact that one person dies from a smoking-related disease every four minutes in the UK and that some of those people will only be in their middle years may not unduly bother a 15-year-old but she could, perhaps, be persuaded of the harm she is doing to her short-term health and how this can impact on her academic progress. She will be more prone to wheeziness and shortness of breath and susceptible to respiratory diseases which will keep her off school. She also needs to know that women who smoke often find it more difficult to conceive and are more likely to have premature babies.

If all else fails, you should try to reduce the amount of money your child has to spend on cigarettes. A drastic cutback in pocket money may be the only way to at least reduce the number of cigarettes she is smoking each day. You could also sit down with her and go through the figures on just how much smoking addiction costs and how many CDs or clothes could be bought for the same amount.

Alcohol abuse

The figures on under-age drinking are enough to make any parent fearful for their child. Research carried out in 2002 revealed that 18 per cent of 11 to 15-year-olds admitted to drinking alcohol at least once a week.

It is not surprising that children find alcohol appealing. It is readily available and you yourself may think it the acceptable face of substance abuse and be far less concerned than if you discovered your child was using illegal drugs. We are bombarded with advertisements for alcohol, many of which suggest that we can't have a good time without it. Enormous amounts of alcohol appear to be consumed by characters in our favourite soaps, where the pub is depicted as the social centre of the community. The message conveyed is that it is all right to get drunk now and again, that the whole thing is just a bit of fun.

Most of us drink alcohol at some time in our lives. For centuries it has been an accepted accompaniment to celebrations and festivals and taken in moderation it is undeniably one of the great pleasures of life. Taking draconian measures and grounding your child if you find he has been drinking is likely to be counterproductive. This will simply make it just a more daring, and therefore more attractive, proposition for an adolescent. You have to accept that your child lives in a world where alcohol is readily available and acceptable, and as a parent your task is to demonstrate how to drink sensibly. One way to do this is to allow him 'tasters' at home so that he can initially discover the effects it has on him in the safe environment of home. You might offer him a glass of wine at a family gathering, perhaps watered down in the form of a spritzer. Never drink excessively in front of your child or regale people with stories of your own youthful drunken experiences in his presence. Your child needs to know what the limits are and this is best done by your own example. You could also point out that, regularly consumed, alcohol can lead to weight gain and related health disorders such as diabetes and heart problems.

It is reassuring to know that while almost all adolescents experiment at some point with alcohol the majority do not turn into alcoholics. Like smoking, drinking is seen as a sign of being grown up, but he needs to be aware of how dangerous alcohol can be if not handled sensibly. When a child starts drinking he will be unable to judge his limits; he has lower amounts of water in his smaller body to help dilute the alcohol so he will feel the effects quickly. He needs to know just how much damage can be caused by a loss of control.

Peer pressure is a major factor in under-age drinking and your child may choose to take risks rather than appear a wimp to his friends. More confident children are able to refuse to get involved in something they don't want to do; once again, self-esteem plays a large part.

There are several signs which may indicate that your child is abusing alcohol. He may have less appetite at the dinner table and prefer to snack rather than eat regular meals. He may also suddenly lose interest in his schoolwork or become less enthusiastic about sports and hobbies on which he was once very keen. You may detect a new moodiness which is more extreme than the usual teenage angst and he may even become uncharacteristically aggressive towards you.

If a child does continue to drink, especially if he is doing so in secret, it suggests that there may be serious problems in his life which the alcohol is helping to dull. Perhaps he is finding it difficult to make friends or is being bullied at school. Perhaps he is concerned about his sexual identity. Encouraging your child to talk about his problems can be difficult at this stage in his life, even if you have previously had a close, loving relationship. It may be necessary to enlist the help of other members of the family, such as older siblings or a favourite uncle. You should also talk to his teachers about your suspicions as the individual school culture can greatly influence this type of destructive behaviour. Parents of his peer group can also be supportive in ensuring that alcohol is not available at parties and that the drinks cupboard is kept firmly locked when young teenagers are left alone in the house.

Illegal drug use

As a parent you may tolerate some smoking and drinking in your adolescent as long as it doesn't get out of hand, but you are likely to react in a very different way if you discover your child is sniffing solvents or taking cannabis.

No parents can afford to be complacent about the drugs risk. Both soft and hard drugs are readily accessible on our streets, perhaps even in the school playground. Boys are more likely to experiment than girls and often this is out of curiosity; they just want to see what it is like. Even quite young children are reasonably well informed about drugs so it is essential that parents become equally knowledgeable. Children often assume that their parents know nothing about what is going on and can, therefore, be easily duped. On the other hand, if you experimented with an illegal drug during your own youth, it's best to be honest about it. The fact that it is something Mum or Dad has tried may actually help to make drug-taking less appealing!

While we tend to talk about drugs in a very general way there are so many different types, and their effects and the dangers can vary considerably. Here we discuss those substances which are most likely to be available to your adolescent.

Solvent abuse

Sniffing or inhaling glue, gas aerosols or other solvents are most common in the early teens. Glue is put into a bag and the fumes inhaled. Lighter fuel is usually inhaled straight from the canister. The effects on the child are similar to alcohol in that it makes her feel light-headed and uninhibited. The dangers of this behaviour cannot be overemphasized. A number of people have died almost instantly from solvent abuse, long before medical help can reach them.

The long-term use of solvents can cause temporary, and sometimes permanent, brain damage as well as damage to the liver and kidneys. Users often become overtired and forgetful or suffer depression. Other signs that your child may be indulging in solvent abuse are a rash around the mouth, unco-ordinated movements and slurred speech. He may go off his food and complain of frequent headaches or stomach cramps.

Cannabis

This is the most widely used and best known drug in the UK and users tend to come from a very wide age range, including the mature adult. Cannabis, also known as marijuana, is a green, brown or grey mixture of dried, shredded flowers and leaves from the hemp plant. It is usually smoked in a cigarette or 'joint' or in a pipe. In small amounts it may have very little effect, although if it is eaten the effects will be longer lasting. Our society tends to send out ambivalent messages about the dangers of cannabis and many liberally minded people argue that it is a harmless drug which should be legalized. Indeed, it is sometimes prescribed by doctors to relieve the pain of patients suffering from certain chronic conditions.

The effects of cannabis vary from person to person and depend on the situation in which the drug is being used. The user may find it helps them to feel happier and more relaxed, but they may in the long term suffer from anxiety and paranoia and have memory problems. A fatal overdose of cannabis is virtually impossible and many believe that smoking cannabis is less harmful than tobacco. However, persistent users are likely to suffer from the same types of respiratory diseases, including lung cancer.

If you find items such as pipes or cigarette papers, which are used for rolling joints, hidden away in your teenager's bedroom or if you detect an unfamiliar smell on his clothes, the chances are he is using cannabis. It is not a physically addictive drug but your child may find it increasingly difficult to cope in social situations without it. There is also the risk that having begun with cannabis he will go on to try harder and more dangerous drugs.

Ecstasy, amphetamines and LSD

These are the types of drugs your child is likely to come across once he starts going out to parties and clubs. Young people are enticed into using these drugs in the belief that they will help them to have a better time and behave more confidently. Peer pressure is a very strong issue here. The danger with some of these substances is that they can be administered to someone without his knowledge, for instance slipped into a drink.

Ecstasy is a stimulant which comes in the form of a tablet, which sometimes even bears a designer logo to make it appear more desirable. The effects are immediate. The user feels happy and energetic, able to go on dancing all night. It is dangerous because if he doesn't take breaks and drink plenty of water or other non-alcoholic drinks he will become dehydrated and collapse. There have been several well-publicized deaths from the effects of ecstasy but many young people seem able to cope with occasional use. However, if it is used long term, it can cause mental health problems and liver and kidney damage.

LSD, known as 'acid', is a clear, tasteless powder, taken by mouth. The effects become evident between 30 and 90 minutes after taking it. The pupils dilate, and body temperature, heart rate and blood pressure increase. The drug can also cause delusions and hallucinations, known as a 'trip', which can be terrifying to the user and cause panic. The effects of an LSD trip can take hours to disperse and sometimes flashbacks occur without warning months or even years later. LSD is an extremely dangerous drug which can lead to severe mental illness and depression.

Amphetamines or 'speed' comes in the form of a grey or white powder which is usually taken dissolved in a drink. Initially it helps the user feel more confident and full of energy. It also acts as an appetite suppressant so has been used misguidedly in the past to help people lose weight. We know now that amphetamines are dangerously addictive and should be avoided at all costs.

There is no failsafe way of preventing your child from ever experimenting with drugs, but it is essential that you recognize the signs of use and, if necessary, seek help before it is too late. What is important is that you always maintain the lines of communication even when you feel totally rejected. Make sure that your child feels you are actively involved and interested in his life, not just in his progress at school or college, but also where and with whom he is spending his leisure time. The child who becomes seriously addicted to drugs is usually someone who is using them to help him cope with personal problems when he feels there is nobody there for him in whom he can confide.

8

The couch potato, loss of interest in sport, activities to do together

Once children reach adolescence society seems to conspire against them to turn them into couch potatoes. Most sports initiatives within schools and local councils are aimed at younger children, the idea being to get them into good habits while they are young, while teenagers are left with little in the way of acceptable physical activity to participate in, unless they are passionate about a particular sport and play as part of a school or college team.

Motivating the couch potato

If you take a look at the season's timetable at your local swimming pool or sports centre you will see plenty of activities for the over-50s, sessions for pregnant women, classes for pre-schoolers, but probably nothing to entice teenagers to get moving. Your child may have outgrown organizations like the Scouts, Guides and other youth groups, which would have provided opportunities to play sport and be active and even if he hasn't he probably won't want to risk being seen as uncool by his peers.

So, before you launch in with an attempt to harangue your teenager from her position on the couch, surrounded by snacks, drinks, her mobile phone and the remote control, ask yourself what it is that you are suggesting she might get up and do. Vague, negative suggestions, like 'why do you never go for a walk with your friends?' or 'you could join the tennis club down the road' would, you must admit, sound like accusations if they were levelled at you by your mother or one of your friends.

Furthermore, you cannot expect your adolescent to share in the anxiety you may feel for her health and well-being in the long term. Think back – did you worry you might die of a heart attack before you reached pensionable age when you were 16 years old? It's unreasonable to expect a teenager to view his youth as a preparation for middle and old age and it would be sad if he were to do so. That said, there is growing medical evidence to suggest that due to their 'couch potato lifestyle' adolescents are now succumbing to what has always been known as 'adult onset' diabetes, and the 'cellular middle-aged burn-out'– when the body loses its fight to produce enough insulin to control blood sugar levels – that doctors are used to diagnosing in older people is now occurring in unfit adolescents.

The most likely motivation that will get teenagers to rise from the couch and let go of the remote control is to appeal to their vanity, but even this must be handled with kid gloves to avoid damaging their fragile self-esteem. The easiest way to attempt this is actually to tune in yourself to what is being watched on TV and read about in magazines. Instead of criticizing the reality TV show they are glued to, it might be more useful to comment carefully on participants who are obviously fit and confident, or the opposite, and pick up on your child's observations as well. The cult of the celebrity, which is so seductive for teenagers, is also fertile ground in which to sow seeds of reason. Many superstars, male and female, let it be known that they practise yoga several hours a day or work out in the gym with a personal trainer to achieve their finely honed physiques. While you obviously don't want to encourage your child to adopt such a narcissistic and unrealistic attitude, there is definitely an opportunity here to bring up the subject of yoga classes, the gym, or whatever activity is 'big' at the moment. Suspend your distaste for current fashion, music and style if you have to and get into the habit of understanding what is going on and discussing the subjects your child is interested in and of asking questions that are not loaded with criticism. This will help to break down the barriers that encourage children to spend so much time in front of the TV and computer on their own and, ultimately, will chip away at all the 'couch potato time' your child spends.

You could introduce several house rules in order to prevent 'couch potato' syndrome from taking firm hold, and stick to them. First of all, you should endeavour to keep to set mealtimes and these meals should be eaten around the table (as we've discussed in detail in previous chapters). It is easy to let things slide when children start pleading they have homework to do, or a favourite programme to watch, but if you do you should not be surprised when your child resorts to constant snacking and eating at all hours. Second, limit the number of TV sets that you have in your house. If there is a screen in every room family members will start to watch alone and you will be less likely to communicate and keep your children moving. Third, cut down the amount of snacks you buy and make rules about where snacks and drinks can be eaten, for instance not in the bedrooms. Lastly, you may have to consider sacrificing some of your own favourite TV programmes in order to get your child into the habit of sitting down with you and discussing what is on offer and what you can watch together – this will help you limit the amount of time spent on the sofa and, hopefully, bring about a more discerning attitude in your child towards what she watches.

Loss of interest in sport

The thing about lying around glued to the TV or playing computer games obsessively is that it becomes a habit that is hard to break away from. Sitting in a comfortable, warm room, possibly with drawn curtains, can have a numbing, sedative effect. Passing time is hardly noticed and the effort that would have to be made to get up and go out is just too great. After a few weeks of this it is unlikely that anyone would suddenly have a desire to rush out and run around, playing sport or engaging in physical activity of any kind.

Even if your teenager has not succumbed to this scenario it is quite likely that she will have lost interest in sport and physical activity in general, just when she has reached the stage of needing it most. 'Impact exercise' that includes walking or running helps to increase bone mass and prevent osteoporosis in later life. Engaging in sport is also likely to deter children from taking up smoking and drinking to excess. Aerobic activity, in addition to all the obvious benefits of preventing heart disease and some cancers, helps to improve circulation and can be beneficial in combating the dreaded teenage affliction of spots and acne, as well as lifting low moods. However, if your teenager has turned away from sport it is doubtful that he will be moved by being informed of the advantages he is losing out on.

Walk fit

A new approach to physical activity is required to get your child back on track. Given that your child is already likely to be receptive to palm-sized technology, a pedometer may be just the thing to get her moving again. This little 'gadget' is smaller than the palm of your hand and comes with an integral clip to attach to your waistband. Pedometers can be set to record the number of steps you take, the calories you use up, or used as a stopwatch and lap timer. Once you convince your child that walking a mile uses up the same amount of energy as running a mile and is just as effective in the health stakes, both of which are true, you might also like to point out that the optimal level of exercise each day is around 10,000 steps. If you and your teenager both wear a pedometer (they are very inexpensive to buy), you can compare how many steps it takes to walk to the video shop or go shopping and you may find the habit quite compulsive. Most pedometers come with a booklet to record steps taken each day and give advice on weight maintenance and loss. You can adjust the pedometer to take account of your individual stride and weight and so, if you wish, work out how many calories you should consume each day in order to maintain or lose weight, given that 20 steps equals one calorie burned. If your child takes to this easy and currently 'cool' method of exercising you might also care to mention that in order to counteract the effects of a Big Mac, large fries and large drink you would have to take 20,000 steps. A pedometer is, if nothing else, a good awareness-raising ploy.

Gym fit

Going to the gym was, until recently, classed as an adult occupation, but fitness companies have been quick to pick up on the general concern about youth fitness, or rather the lack of it, and have responded accordingly. The concerns about allowing 'young adults' to use gym circuits have always centred on the fact that teenagers' bodies are still developing and growing and it is easy to strain muscles or build inappropriate bulk. There is also the psychological aspect of encouraging children to aspire to some unattainable ideal of physical perfection that will dog them for the rest of their lives. However, the change in attitude and practice within the gym environment counteracts these fears. Most gyms these days do not focus entirely on weight training and most provide a wide variety of classes, as well as nutritional advice and one-to-one guidance if and when it is required. The gym could well be the answer for the unfit teenager who is completely turned off by the great outdoors and loathes sport.

What to look for in a gym

- Many gyms provide family membership and/or discounted rates for students and those under the age of 21 – this is well worth considering as gym membership can be very expensive.
- The gym should have staff that your child can relate to and feel comfortable with but who should also be helpful and well-informed as far as you are concerned.
- The gym should offer plenty of alternatives – swimming

73

pool, kick boxing studio, circuit training, different classes. Find out what attracts your child and make sure it is all under one roof.

- The gym should be located near to your home. If your child has to rely on a lift from you whenever she wants to use the gym she will be limited as to when she can go, even if you intend to join with her.

- Beware the gym with the ultra-sophisticated clientele – this can be daunting for teenagers. Pop in a couple of times before signing the joining form to ensure the place is not overcrowded at the time your child would use it.

- Consider school and college gyms – many are opening their doors to outsiders as commercial ventures. They are cheaper than private gyms but do not offer so many facilities.

Martial arts

Disciplines like karate, judo and tai kwon do all lend themselves to family participation. If your child is reluctant to go along on his own or is worried about being singled out for attention in a class, you should definitely consider a martial arts class. The advantage of this type of class is that there are likely to be other families participating, so your child will not feel awkward about being accompanied by you and will be able to receive the support he needs from your being there.

Ideally, you should look for a class that is new to both of you – learning and practising together will help to boost your child's morale and is preferable to him being the novice and you being in the position that you are always in, of knowing more than he does. You may find that learning a physical art together has all kinds of beneficial side-effects: your adolescent may be going through a stage of finding it difficult to communicate with you and you with him, but now you will have something in common and a neutral topic to discuss. You will get to spend time with your child, even if he is trying to throw you across his shoulder, when you are out of the house, away from possible points of conflict, and you can enjoy a healthy pastime together as you probably did when he was younger.

This type of class is something that you can do together at a relatively low cost, but you should still both go along to one or more classes before making a commitment. On the subject of commitment, you must remember that your role in taking a class or joining a club primarily lies in helping your child to overcome his demotivation towards sport and being fit. When your child reaches the stage where it is obvious he would rather continue alone or with friends his own age then it is time for you to bow out. If there is more than one class per week, you could make the tactful excuse that is easier for you to attend the class your child is not in, to relieve her of any embarrassment she might feel about approaching this subject, or you may have to sacrifice the class completely to ensure that your child goes on unhampered. You can always try a different class or another activity and be proud of the fact that you have succeeded in rekindling your child's enthusiasm for exercise.

Aerobics

Aerobics classes appeal to those who have turned their backs on sport and activity in general because when you take part you can usually make as much or as little effort as you feel you can manage. Classes welcome all ages (from mid-teens upwards), all body shapes and, increasingly, male as well as female. If your child is self-conscious she can hide at the back, but this embarrassment usually subsides after a couple of weeks, especially if the music suits her and the teacher is lively. Aerobics classes gained a poor reputation a while back because of unskilled teaching and the injuries that resulted from that. However, there are now recognized qualifications for teachers and it is easy to check up on this when you choose which class to go to. Warming up and cooling down stretches should form part of the class and you should be asked about your medical history and any injuries before taking part. Choosing a class with no more than 15 participants makes it easier to grasp the moves and ensures you have room to try them out properly.

Too low to move?

Not all teenagers will allow themselves to be shifted off the couch or encouraged to join a class or go to the gym, but this doesn't mean that you can or should give up on them. If you are certain that the habit of lying around is just that – a habit and not a symptom of a more debilitating psychological condition (see the next chapter) – then you may have to take more drastic action. If your child won't go to the gym, perhaps you could bring the gym to your child in the form of one or two pieces of equipment – a treadmill or exercise bike, for example, could be used at the same time as watching TV or listening to music.

The upside to such an arrangement is that your child would not have to leave the house and so, in theory, could use the equipment whenever he wants, but this means that the equipment has to be positioned where it is readily accessible and can't be ignored. Before you convert your garage to a home gym, ask yourself if anyone is really going to go out there in the depths of winter? The downside lies in the fact that the number of items of gym equipment you see regularly advertised in local papers and on noticeboards must mean that these things end up not being used. However, if you and your child agree, and you do need a firm agreement that whatever you buy will be used, this is also an advantage, in that you can obtain equipment at not too great an expense.

A more drastic solution for the reluctant mover could be to organize a class or even a youth group yourself. It has been said before that most facilities simply do not cater for teenagers, so perhaps it is time to provide some of your own. You could rent a badminton court to try and entice your adolescent and a few of her friends to run around in relative privacy, or you could buy a table-tennis table, if you have space at home. Most people are unaware of how demanding this Olympic sport can be at the 'fun' level and even teenagers who have turned their backs on all physical activity might find it hard to resist.

One of the most life-changing solutions is to buy a dog. Almost all children, even teenagers, would love to own a dog, if they don't already have one, and this is a sure-fire way of getting everyone out walking. Before you broach the subject, you must be certain that you can definitely afford to have one, in terms of the extra expense and the time the animal will demand. Dogs should not be left alone all day and need constant care and attention, so this is a high commitment option and not something to be taken lightly. However, it is also extremely rewarding in terms of the satisfaction you and your children will receive from having a dog. If your child really wants a dog you must reach a solemn agreement that she will do her share of the walking. There will inevitably be times when that agreement is broken but you will simply have to keep on coming back to it for the sake of everyone's well-being.

9

Lethargy, depression

Teenagers can seem frighteningly lethargic at times. They sit around the house yawning and tend to nap a lot. This can be exasperating for parents who become irritated by what they see as their child's excessive laziness. Be assured that this is most likely to be normal teenage behaviour and if he springs to life the minute the telephone rings for him or friends come visiting there is very little to worry about.

However, if he is so lethargic that he can no longer be bothered to take part in his favourite sport or go out to social events this may be a sign that he is becoming seriously depressed, and then there is very real cause for concern.

You need to be as mindful of your child's mental and emotional health as you are about his physical well-being. The two are so closely interrelated that it is almost impossible to function properly if either one needs attention. The child who feels bad about himself, who finds it difficult to make friends or feels unloved is unlikely to be enthusiastic about creating his own fitness programme, healthy eating and other life-enhancing activities. He will be more inclined to indulge in things which give him a quick fix of happiness but which can actually do him harm, like eating too much junk food, smoking, drinking or even taking drugs.

Most teenagers have occasional feelings of gloom and doom – times when they hide themselves away in the bedroom or refuse to speak to anyone. These are common feelings in adolescence which need not concern you if they are passing phases. But as parents you need to recognize what might be much more serious – when depression goes beyond the normal teenage angst. You will not always know what is going on in your child's life now he is a teenager; he is more likely to confide in his friends than in you, which means that you will not necessarily be aware of his feelings and the depth of his distress.

It has been estimated that between 15 and 20 per cent of adolescents suffer some kind of mental disorder. A significant number experience serious psychological problems, and illnesses such as schizophrenia usually begin to manifest themselves at this stage. Over the past few decades there has been increasing concern about the growth of depression in children and young people and the fact that the incidence of suicide in teenagers is becoming much more common. The Samaritans report that there has been a marked increase in the incidence of suicide, particularly among young men aged 15 to 24, in the UK since the 1970s. In fact, suicide ranks as one of the most common causes of death in the teens and early twenties, and has taken over from road accidents as the main cause of death for adult males under the age of 24.

There is a gender difference. Girls usually find it easier to talk about their feelings with their parents, friends or teachers and, although more young girls appear to suffer from depression, young men are at the most risk of suicide. Any threat to kill themselves should always be taken seriously and medical help sought.

Some of these suicides are believed to be related to alcohol or substance abuse, which affects the ability to reason and causes depression. However, in general, adolescents who attempt to take their own lives appear to grow up in families with more than their fair share of turmoil. The trauma of sexual abuse which has occurred at an earlier age can impact very strongly when adolescence is reached and a child becomes much more aware of the implications. Whatever bad things are causing the extreme emotional distress, the adolescent lacks adequately developed skills for coping with it alone.

Depressive illness in children and teens is defined when the feelings of depression persist and interfere with a child's or adolescent's ability to function. Never ridicule any statement such as 'I want to kill myself', or 'I'm going to commit suicide.' Changing the subject or telling the child not to be silly is not helpful. He may not be prepared to carry out the threat, although you can never be sure, but it is quite likely he is trying to make you understand how unhappy he is. However busy you are, you cannot afford to dismiss what he has said. It is best to grasp the moment and find out exactly why your child is feeling so desperate.

It is also worth noting that depression tends to run in families, so if a parent or grandparent has been a sufferer your child is at more risk.

Signs of depression

There are a number of signals which should alert you to the fact that your child could be seriously depressed.

Your normally confident child may suddenly become quiet and withdrawn. He seems to lose interest in those activities which he previously enjoyed – even football may no longer have any interest for him and he may complain about vague aches and pains or experience light-headedness or dizziness.

His physical appearance may change. He may look pale and miserable all the time, seem tearful or burst into tears for no apparent reason. He might seem to lack all motivation and may be unable to concentrate even on watching television or reading a magazine. His schoolwork begins to suffer. He may be too apathetic to do his homework or appear simply not to care any more what kind of grades he gets.

Many young teenagers are not too careful about personal hygiene, but be aware of any sudden changes in behaviour: the child who previously spent hours in the bathroom but is now careless about showering or changing his clothes, may be sinking into depression.

He may also find it difficult to relate to family and friends and try to avoid family gatherings and celebrations. Fights and arguments with brothers and sisters may go far beyond normal sibling rivalry. The young person who used to see his friends a lot may now seem to prefer to be alone most of the time. He feels isolated because he does not believe that anyone could be as unhappy as he is. This may be particularly true if a child is confused about his sexual identity and is terrified that someone may find out. At the time in his life when he desperately wants to be one of the crowd, anything which makes him feel different from his friends is likely to cause unhappiness.

Being overweight can also be the cause of your child's depression. As we have already discussed, one of the social consequences of obesity is that children are often bullied and alienated from their peers.

The depressed child will feel like a failure in all areas of his life and have negative views about his competence and self-worth. Some children find the demands of the education system overwhelming; in the UK they take far more exams than they used to and continued full-time education, after the legal school-leaving age is reached, may not necessarily be the right thing for your child. If you have unrealistic academic expectations for him this will obviously increase the sense of failure. This may make your child become very irritable and hostile towards you. In extreme cases he may feel so rejected that he tries running away from home. This is usually a cry for help and may be the first time that parents realize that their child has a problem and needs help.

Depression is a real illness and early diagnosis and treatment is essential. Your child will require professional help as well as lots of support from family and friends. The type of treatment he receives should be comprehensive, involving both individual and family therapy, and, possibly, some medication. Some antidepressants which have been commonly prescribed to help young people with depression are now believed to actually increase the risk of suicide and self-harm. Although there are concerns about certain medications, most mental health professionals continue to recommend their use for children who are severely depressed. You should discuss any fears you have about this with your doctor before he prescribes.

Self-harming

Teens who have difficulty talking about their feelings may show their emotional tension, physical discomfort, pain and low self-esteem with self-injurious behaviours, such as cutting. It sounds perverse, but inflicting physical injuries on herself helps a child who is unhappy to feel temporarily better, particularly if she is someone who finds it difficult to talk about her anger or fears. The Samaritans have described self-harming as 'like screaming without opening your mouth'. It releases emotion and helps them to feel in control. The triggers for self-harming can be bullying, a bereavement in the family, exam stress or physical or sexual abuse. According to Childline, the number of children calling about self-harming has rapidly increased in the last decade, as has the number of people attending A&E departments with self-inflicted injuries. However, this may be because nowadays people feel more able to be open about it. The most common age for self-harming is between 12 and 15 but it has been identified in children as young as five.

Nine out of ten of these self-harmers are girls. It has sometimes been described as attention-seeking, but in fact it is usually something carried out in secret, either in the bedroom or bathroom at home or in the toilets at school.

Sleep

The average 12 to 13-year-old sleeps for nine and a half hours, but of course all children are different. If you are concerned that your child isn't getting sufficient sleep, keep a record over the next few weeks. If he seems to be having around nine to ten hours per night, and is lively and alert the next day, there should be no cause for concern. There may be some slight variations. Some nights he'll sleep more, on others less, but he will easily make up for a lost hour or so over subsequent nights.

Many teenagers can be difficult to rouse in the morning,

although more boys than girls tend to suffer from morning sleepiness. It has been suggested that the biological rhythms in adolescence are not suited to early-morning waking and in some parts of the USA they have even delayed the school start time to accommodate their high school pupils!

Difficulty in getting to sleep or disturbed sleep does not necessarily indicate that your child is depressed. In fact, sleep deprivation is a common problem in people of all ages these days. We now have a 24-hour day: television and radio programmes run throughout the night, there is the constant hum of traffic if you live in a town and street lighting can be very intrusive. Many of us are finding it difficult to wind down at the end of the day.

As we have already discussed, a certain amount of lethargy and sleepiness is normal in the teenage years, but if your child is staying up late at night and finding it difficult to get up for school in the morning you need to take a firm hand and try to help him develop a healthier sleep pattern.

Developing a sleep routine

If your child is obese, he will probably be more susceptible to sleep disturbances. Obesity causes a condition known as sleep apnoea which means that breathing ceases momentarily during sleep. The most common cause is the over-relaxation of the soft palate muscles in the throat. Each pause lasts around ten seconds and the child may not even be aware that this is happening, although sometimes it may wake him up momentarily. While he will probably remember nothing about this the following morning he is likely to suffer from excessive sleepiness. This, in turn, will make him feel too tired to take physical exercise. The only solution to this problem is for him to lose weight and increase his level of fitness.

Interestingly, sleep deprivation may even be part of the obesity problem. One study has shown that lack of sleep has a detrimental effect on the hormone leptin, which controls appetite. The theory is that when someone sleeps badly, the leptin levels are lowered and send a false message to the brain that the body needs more calories, resulting in overeating.

Routine is the crucial element in getting a good night's sleep. When your child was younger he probably went to bed at the same time each night. The established pattern of bath, bedtime story, then a goodnight kiss and lights out helped him to settle down happily for the night.

Once a child reaches his teens, getting him off to bed can become a real battle, especially if, as his parents, you are desperate for him to go to his room and allow you to have some time to yourselves. If he senses you are keen for him to be out of the way he may even be more determined to delay his bedtime! Be realistic, though. While it's good to be firm, it's no use expecting your 14-year-old to go to bed at the same time as he did at the age of ten. Encouraging him to read in bed may help him to fall asleep and allow you to have some time alone with your partner.

The battle at bedtime will be worth it if you can finally help him understand that a regular bedtime – going to bed and getting up at roughly the same time every day – is essential if he is to perform well at school, play a full part in his favourite sport and enjoy all his social activities to the full. Be prepared to allow a little more flexibility at weekends and during school holidays but do retain some routine or he will find it very difficult to revert to early nights and early mornings when term begins again.

Some very simple adjustments can make all the difference to the quality of your child's sleep. First, cut out tea and coffee before bedtime and offer a milky drink, such as hot chocolate, instead. Eat dinner a little earlier in the evening so you allow several hours between his last meal and bedtime.

You could put up black-out curtains in his room to cut out intrusive, outside lighting and you may have to invest in a new bed. If he has a child-sized bed this may be the time for a change. Someone who is growing taller and broader every day may be more comfortable in a double bed, if there is room for it.

You could try to make going to bed a pleasant shared experience, as it was when he was younger. He may be too old to enjoy a bedtime story but if you can spare some time to sit on his bed and chat about his day it will help him to feel calm and relaxed at the pre-sleep stage and you should gain more insight into what is happening in his life. With the right encouragement he can use the opportunity to talk about anything which might be worrying him.

If he still isn't ready to sleep allow him to read for as long as he wants, within reason, but ban the playing of loud music or watching television. You need to establish a quiet, calm atmosphere prior to sleep.

This can be difficult with current lifestyles. The function of the child's bedroom used to be primarily for sleeping but now it is just as likely to be a study and an entertainment centre. Recent research from MINTEL showed that 11 to 14-year-olds have replaced family living with technology-filled bedrooms. Three-quarters of children of this age have a television in their bedroom, almost two-thirds have their own DVD player or video recorder, and a quarter have a computer. All this can cause over-stimulation and hardly makes the room conducive to rest and relaxation.

If your child is having serious sleep problems you should put the television or computer in another room to avoid the temptation of late-night viewing or computer games. He may also find it very hard to wind down if he has been studying for exams all day in the same room. Once again, if possible, try to reorganize so that he has his desk and books in another part of the house. Most children have far more exams to pass than their parents did but you must try to guard against excessive studying. Hours spent over books will not help your child to succeed and overtiredness will make getting to sleep much more difficult. Help him to draw up a study plan which allows two-hour sessions of work, followed by a break and time off to go for a walk or engage in some other form of physical exercise so that he can switch off for a while. This may be more difficult than you think to implement, as over-anxious children will not be keen to spend any time away from their desk. Indulge him by keeping him topped up with drinks of water and being as loving and understanding as you can be, even when faced with a really irritable son.

Learning relaxing techniques such as yoga or meditation will help alleviate the stress and help your child to wind down before bedtime. In fact this is something you could do together.

Try not to become over-anxious about the quality of your child's sleep as this will be communicated to him; he will start worrying himself about going to sleep and will consequently find it even harder to drop off.

If sleep problems persist your child may need professional help. Encouraging him to keep a sleep diary over a period of two weeks or so may give you more insight into the causes. For instance, if he sleeps much better and seems adequately rested on non-school days, it may be worries about his academic work or something like bullying which are keeping him awake at night. Such a diary can also provide the information your doctor needs to help him decide on appropriate treatment or whether it is necessary to refer your child to a sleep specialist.

10

The future, eating together, refusing to be influenced by the media, taking a moral stand

There is some good news. The world's largest hamburger chain has abandoned its 'supersize' menu option, introduced salads on to the bill of fare and has revealed imminent plans for a 'healthy' sandwich range. The food and drink industry is responding to widespread concern over childhood obesity by withdrawing 'king size' chocolate bars and reviewing the salt and fat content of tinned products such as soups. A casual glance at the newspapers on any given week will alert you to the fact that the World Health Organization, our own government and medical bodies are all now agreed on the need for action concerning the future health and well-being of our children. This type of blanket coverage of a problem can, of course, have the opposite of the desired affect. People can be induced to feel that everyone's health and fitness will be taken care of by outside forces, or that when a problem is so widespread it is hopeless to try and tackle it. It is almost feasible, when you look around you, to accept overweight as being the norm – together with the subsequent health risks. It can seem as if it is everyone's problem and nobody's responsibility.

You control your family's health

The answer lies, though, in ignoring the mood of panic and focusing closer to home. Once you accept that the key to your own family's fitness and good health lies in your and their hands you can start to employ a matter-of-fact, long-term approach to your family's future health and well-being that is sure to win through. Remember that even if your local council buys back land for school playing fields and promotes the latest concept of healthy, balanced meals in school canteens – like smart card incentive schemes that issue bonus points when they're used to buy healthy food – the foundation for your child's fit, healthy body and life is laid down and built upon at home.

You should also accept that your child is likely to receive hundreds, if not thousands, of pieces of advice on diet, health and fitness by the time she reaches adolescence, from well-meaning friends, teachers and relatives. In addition to this, there is likely to be a constant bombardment of celebrity-inspired diet and fitness 'news' items circulating on the internet, TV and through magazines and newspapers. Now you know what you are up against you may wish you could take your family to live on a desert island that is free from all negative influences; but the answer lies not in switching off from all these pressures upon your child, but in tuning into them and using them to help you maintain the sensible balance in her life that she needs.

Celebrity diets, bizarre exercise regimes, one star's anorexia, another's ballooning weight problem, can all form part of your family's dinner table talk, if you retain a calm exterior and a sense of humour. Any attempt to ban your child completely from watching TV, using the internet or perusing magazines is doomed to failure and is likely to alienate her from her peers and cause more problems than it could ever solve. Similarly, vocal and outright condemnation of all the fads and foibles that you know to be ridiculous and, in some cases, downright unhealthy and dangerous, will only teach your child to discuss these matters elsewhere and with others who may not have such a sensible perspective. Encouraging your child to acquaint herself with the diets and lifestyles that are described so extensively in the media, and helping her to make a reasoned judgement on the validity of what she discovers, is much more likely to deflate the exaggerated and unhelpful claims that seem to surface every month, if not every week, than if you stridently deride everything and everyone connected with this issue.

Family meals

Family mealtimes have been mentioned throughout this book. This is because they are the glue that helps to bind your family together and they provide your child with her basic nutritional needs. Once adolescence is reached, eating together can often appear to add to the friction that is already there in the house and the dinner table can become the meeting ground for arguments between siblings and parents. The answer lies in perseverance. If disputes centre around who is going to clear up afterwards, work out a rota and post it on the refrigerator; if quarrels break out over what is being eaten, make a note to discuss the 'menu' with the chief offenders before the next meal, or canvas ideas and practical help from everyone in order to foster their involvement and squash their excuses for absenting themselves.

Learn to ride the storm and try to introduce neutral or humorous subjects during mealtimes to diffuse building tensions. Gathering together as a family to eat is a habit, and a good one. If you persist with serving meals at set times each day your children will simply accept it as part of their routine. Inevitably you will meet with rebellion – your teenager may simply be out at a mealtime or your younger child may spoil the mood by refusing to eat what's put in front of him – but these hiccups do not mean that you should abandon this civilized and civilizing habit. Family mealtimes can help imbue your child with a healthy attitude towards food, they can ensure that your child is properly nourished and they can even, if you are lucky, bring about some of the best memories of family life.

A balanced attitude

It is imperative that, while you are busy encouraging your child to eat at the table with you, you do not accidentally instil a guilty attitude towards food. There can be few of us who have not, at some time or other, heard the off-the-cuff remark 'we should think of the starving children elsewhere in the world' in relation to food being left on the plate. This type of comment is flippant and insulting, but worse, it may, if said often enough, impress upon your child the concept that food is something to feel uncomfortable about and that she should feel guilty because she has enough to eat while others don't. Many overweight people cite being pressured to eat everything up when they were young as the cause of their weight problems, and habits gained in childhood are hard to break. If your child constantly leaves food on her plate then it is up to you to cook and serve less to avoid wasting it. The plight of the world's poor is too heavy a burden to be placed upon your child's shoulders, as is the state of the family's bank balance and the cost of the weekly food bill.

This much said, there is everything to be gained by gently introducing your child to the concept that food doesn't just miraculously appear on the plate, nor does it begin its journey to the plate at the supermarket, but originates from farms and factories, some of which may be on the other side of the world. How far you go with this depends on your own inclinations and beliefs, but, as with everything else connected with food, the key lies in preserving a healthy balance. For example, you could introduce your child to 'Fair Trade' chocolate and explain to her that you buy this product because you know that the producers have been properly paid and treated without exploitation; encourage her to accept that this chocolate (which tastes great) will be bought as a treat once or twice a week, rather than other, cheaper chocolates, which are produced without regard to the cocoa growers. You should not, however, ban your child from eating other treats when she is with friends, or make an enormous fuss if she wants to try other brands once in a while. In other words, chocolate should not be laden with guilt in any shape or form.

Your child is likely to appreciate the implications of Fair Trade more easily if you show him how families, with children just like him, rely on us to buy these products. There is plenty of positive information available about this on Fair Trade websites and in stores which stock these products and, if you are lucky, once your child reaches secondary school your moral choice will be supported by the ethics lessons that are now a part of the national curriculum.

Food shopping and preparation

Closer to home, but no less important, there is an increasing number of farmers' markets and community growing schemes blossoming around the country. These markets deserve our support and will help your child to appreciate that real food has nothing to do with the 'bargain bucket', 'eat all you can' ethos that is sold so heavily to the young by fast-food companies. You may not have time to shop daily for your family's food, and no one is advocating a nostalgic replay of the days when women spent a huge amount of every day shopping and preparing food, but this does not mean that you can't take an active interest in what is produced locally and what tastes good. If you occasionally take a stroll, preferably with your child, to your nearest farmers' market or simply to the nearest stalls that sell fresh produce and vegetables, you will be surprised at the variety and quality of food that is available. Simply avoiding the supermarket occasionally also means you are likely to spend less because you will not be loading up a trolley with special offers and other 'bargains' that you probably didn't intend to buy in the first place.

A trip to the farmers' market may be viewed as an enjoyable outing for younger children and older ones can normally be tempted if you combine the market with somewhere else they want to go. There is usually plenty of free tasting and samples on offer in farmers' markets and this can include anything from ostrich burgers to cheese and fruit juice. This type of experience is likely to excite your child's curiosity as well as educate her into the idea that food is something to be relished and there is more to taste and ingredients than fat, sugar and salt. Buying produce from a market may also lead to you and your child spending more time thinking and planning what you will eat and how you will cook it. This in turn is likely to initiate a much healthier attitude towards her overall diet than if she sees her meals coming straight from the freezer to the microwave and on to the plate each day. Even if you can only manage to find time for market shopping and buying once or twice a month it is worth showing your child that there are different options available, and interesting ones at that.

Bear in mind, also, when you are planning a day's outing with your child, or even a holiday, that there are plenty of places that specialize in fresh fish or are famous for a particular cheese. There are also farms and orchards that hold special events to increase interest in their produce, and there are ethnic markets where you can try foods you may not have eaten before. Treat the tasting and the sampling in a low-key manner, as a side-effect of outings and holidays, and remember, the broader your child's experience of food becomes, the less likely she is to experience problems with eating healthily and attaining a balanced lifestyle.

Use the media to your advantage

When you are out shopping with your child you might also like to throw your 'coffee break' into the 'fair trade' equation. Many of the TV sitcoms from the USA that children enjoy are situated in, or regularly feature, characters sitting around in coffee houses. In this country this has translated into coffee house chains springing up on every high street. The coffee companies that own these outlets can be seen to be directly responsible for driving down the price of coffee and keeping families in coffee-producing countries at subsistence level. You can choose, in the same way that you introduce your child to different food retailers, to patronize different cafés and coffee shops when you are enjoying a break with your child. Some town centres now boast snack bars that plough their profits into charities, while almost all have churches that offer coffee and cakes at weekends. If you introduce your child to a different take on everyday events like this you will enrich and widen her vision of the world without ever having to lecture or preach. As your child grows older and meets for coffee at weekends with her friends she is more likely to explore different venues and approach consumerism more objectively in general if you have introduced her to the broader picture.

Perhaps you can also use TV and magazines to foster an interest in the preparation of the food you buy together, by trying out recipes that you see being prepared by TV chefs and cutting out and keeping interesting meal ideas from the press. If you do not usually bother with proper recipes it may seem like a lot of fuss, but if it helps you in encouraging your child to take a lively interest in good food, properly prepared, then it will be worth it, even if you only have time to don the chef's hat once or twice a month.

Home delivery

If time is at a premium for you then you are probably already familiar with the supermarket home delivery service, but if you haven't already done so, you may like to consider having an organic box delivery. Box schemes provide farmers with a dependable outlet for their produce and operate in most areas. The aim is to supply vegetables and fruit in a 'fair, ecological and co-operative' manner, as well as providing a good mix of produce, with the emphasis on what is seasonally available and what is produced locally. Boxes are normally delivered to your door on a weekly basis but you can also arrange to collect your box from the scheme organizer or pick-up point if you prefer.

A mixture of vegetables is usually included and organizers say that children in particular look forward to opening the box each week and finding out what they've been sent. This said, you can opt not to have vegetables that are unpopular in your household and you can order specific vegetables that you prefer. Other items, such as eggs and bread, are often available. The price of a box ranges from around £6.50 and schemes are advertised in local papers and on the internet. If your child is a reluctant vegetable eater then an organic box delivery could be just the thing to ignite her interest.

Many of the growers provide recipes upon request and the delivery person is likely to also be a grower who will be only too happy to chat to you and your child about the produce. Helping your child to appreciate that vegetables aren't harvested in plastic packs, but instead come covered in dirt, may prove a valuable step towards her understanding more about nature and the world around her. Encouraging your child to taste vegetables that have been picked the same day you are going to eat them could engender a lifelong love of good food which is a far cry from the angst-ridden attitude towards eating that many children are destined to grow up with.

Look at other home delivery options, too: you could have bottled mineral water delivered in sparkling or non-sparkling varieties by 'aquaid' companies who use the money they make to support clean water projects in third world countries. If you are always battling with your child over the consumption of fizzy drinks or simply can't get her to drink tap water then this may be an ideal solution. Your local paper, church and community centre will have details of all such food/drink projects that are likely to be of interest to you and your child. Providing your child with a wider perspective on eating and food will be of immense benefit to her in helping her to achieve the balanced attitude that will bring about good health and well-being.

Conclusion

You may sometimes feel that the day your child started school coincided with your loss of control over what she eats and how she views her 'self'. You may also believe that in addition to the influence of her peers, your child has the mighty ranks of the media to contend with and that you are fighting a losing battle against these outside forces that can often seem relentless and overwhelming. It is true that the media is responsible for promoting every eating fad and miracle diet that comes along, but mostly the diets and eating regimes are created not by the newspapers and magazines themselves but by doctors and nutritionists who are searching, as everyone seems to be, for the quick and/or most effective solution to being overweight and unhealthy.

The temptation to succumb to some or all of the quick fixes that are thrown at us can be overwhelming, but realistically we should admit that, as with everything else in life, there is no easy answer, no herbal remedy you can dose your child with to ensure he will always be slim, fit and healthy. The route to achieving good health and fitness for the whole family lies not in any complicated food-combining process or diet that forbids certain foods, or in exercising at certain times of the day or in a particular way. The answer is to stand firm against all the onslaughts and maintain a family approach to fitness and well-being.

This is not an exciting solution, except that you may be surprised at some of the enjoyable 'side-effects' of following up on suggestions we've made in this book. In adopting the routines and advice we put forward you are not likely to receive a standing ovation from your family, but you will have the satisfaction of knowing that you are doing your best for your child.